A Guided Discovery of Gardening

JULIA
ATKINSON-DUNN

A Guided Discovery of Gardening

KNOWLEDGE, CREATIVITY
& JOY UNEARTHED

KOA PRESS

@studiohomegardening / www.studiohome.co.nz

To my partner in creativity, Tonia.
You are the bridge that brings my passion for gardens to these pages.
Our hours spent side by side have been some of the most rewarding of my life.
Thank you.

Conter

ts

My discovery of gardening

Gardening has brought together my passions for writing, research, design and creativity in a way that is wholly consuming. It has forced me to rediscover patience and plugged me back into the cycle of the seasons, learning to work with Mother Nature and all her unpredictable ways!

I had never held much interest in gardening until I moved into my first purchased home in Ōtautahi Christchurch, Aotearoa New Zealand. With an interior designer's eye I viewed the backyard with nervousness, for the first time knowing that I wanted to transform an outside space to meet my visual desires, but also realising that I would begin this adventure without a shred of understanding of how to do that.

Pushed along by the deadlines of my new gardening column for New Zealand's premier news platform, I was constantly seeking gaps in my knowledge that I could answer and share with my readers. My aim has always been to communicate ideas and angles on ornamental gardening from a place of practice, not expertise, as I have come to learn that there is no singular way to use plants – simply our own methods that develop.

Previous page: A springtime view from the back of our garden toward the porch of our villa. **Opposite:** At home in my early autumn garden.

Treat this book as
your trusted friend.
A place you can
return to time and
again for positive
reinforcement as
you embark on
your own journey
of discovering the
beautiful rewards
found in creating
a garden, just
as I have.

A Guided Discovery of Gardening aims to fill in the practical basics needed by beginners while providing inspiration and support for gardeners as they continue to grow in confidence. Through engaging the help of wise green-fingered friends and extracting their valuable advice I've fast tracked my own progress, and through sharing this knowledge I hope I can provide some momentum for your learning, too.

Take inspiration from the featured gardens, picking and choosing snippets of planting to spur on your own. Let the planting concepts and profiles spark fresh perspectives and challenge your preconceived goals.

Treat this book as your trusted friend. A place you can return to time and again for positive reinforcement as you embark on your own journey of discovering the beautiful rewards found in creating a garden, just as I have.

Below: Gathering autumn blooms in my garden. **Next page:** *Verbena bonariensis* interplanted with *Miscanthus sinensis* 'Morning Light' and *Oenothera lindheimeri* (gaura) in the early morning glow.

SECTION ONE

Beginn
guides

er

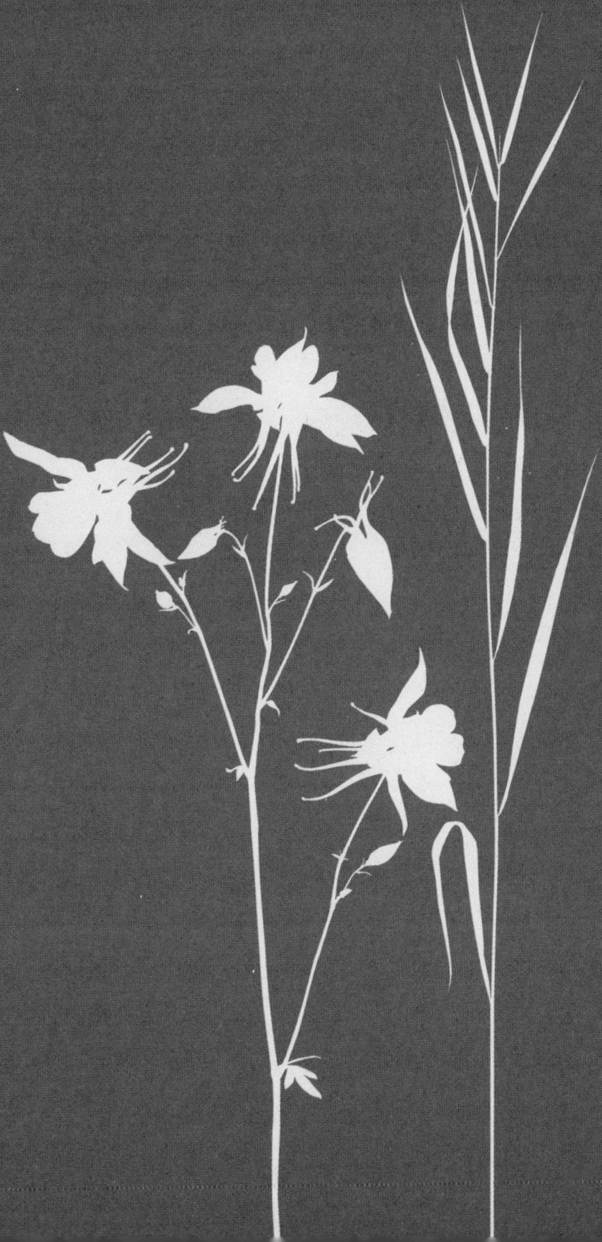

In the following pages,
I break down the baseline
gardening information
that helped me get growing,
and curating my beds
with confidence.

Learn how to propagate
from seed, take cuttings,
divide plants and gain an
understanding of plant types,
the system of botanical
plant names and processes
to create the garden you
envisage.

BEGINNER GUIDES

INEXPLICABLE

Nothing is for nothing.
Everything is rooted,
a branch, an expression
of that to which it belongs.

Everything makes sense
when seen connected.
No aberrations, no mis-steps;
even inexplicable has a place.

- Mary Walker

First published in *The Land Will Hold You* (2022), Castle Press.

Plant types
KNOWLEDGE IS POWER

Having a broad understanding of plant types will unlock your creativity and pathways to further knowledge. The categories over the page are a way to quickly filter plants into groups that explain their growing behaviours and how they interact with the seasons. These are the key to deciding which plants you want to invest in and leave space for, and which plants are in fact not dead but simply disappear over winter!

Once you can identify each plant you love as existing in one of these categories, you are much better prepared to plan your garden, armed with a good understanding of your chosen plants and what will return each year.

This information is also really helpful if you have inherited a garden that you are not yet familiar with. Observe the garden for a full year to see what pops up over the seasons to understand what you are working with, if plants are happy in their location and where they are hiding.

Opposite:
Echinacea purpurea taking centre stage in my summer garden.

PLANT
TYPES

1
PERENNIALS
Herbaceous or woody plants
that regrow, flower and seed
again each year.

2
ANNUALS
Plants that grow, flower,
seed and die in a
single year.

3
BIENNIALS
Plants that complete their
life cycle over two
years, then die.

PERENNIALS

Herbaceous or woody plants that regrow, flower and seed again each year. Some recede down to their roots at the end of the season, while others may stay above ground over winter.

Features of perennials: They can be a terrific investment! If you choose to purchase established plants, you can do so with the knowledge that they will deliver each year and you will be able to collect seed, divide or take cuttings to create more plants to spread around your garden. Some will last for many years (and may also take a few to get going, like peonies). Some may be shorter-lived and start to tire after three years or so.

Tender perennials

These are perennials that won't survive their dormant period in some cold climates, such as those that are severely frost prone or under snow all winter. The best advice is to gauge the conditions where you live, and ask your gardening neighbours what they do.

Bulbs/corms/tubers/rhizomes

These are perennial plants that grow from strange bulbous 'storage organs' of differing types.

Some of these types are hardy (can handle below-freezing temperatures) and some are tender (will die if frosted). They multiply in each growing season, so every two to three years it is worth digging them up, to gently divide and replant your new stock elsewhere. Each type has differing needs regarding when this should be done, so research on your plant may be required.

I'd also advise looking up how to plant each type – I once planted my dahlia tubers upside down and had to dig them up and replant them! Lesson learnt.

Shrubs

These are perennial plants that are smaller than trees but have woody stems above the ground when dormant.

When they go dormant over winter they can either be evergreen, with leaves all year round – such as box hedging, camellias and rhododendrons – or they can be deciduous, where they lose their leaves to reveal their woody stems – such as hydrangeas.

Shrubs are important for flower gardens as they offer structure (page 88) all year round, providing visual interest when your other plants have finished for the year.

ANNUALS

These are plants that grow, flower, seed and die in a single year. Often they are prolific self-seeders and will re-emerge as new plants in the same position.

Features of annuals: They are celebrated for their abundant blooms, especially in summer, and instant brightening- and cheering-up of your outside space. I've found them to be eager, fast growers when planted in their preferred positions, often sunny ones. Many will flower for months if given good care (water, deadheading) and a spot they are happy with.

Annuals can be fantastic for use in hanging planters and pots as well as adding interest to the edges of your garden. You might see annuals being referred to as 'bedding plants' (page 258) at garden centres.

Hardy annuals

These are annuals that can be sown directly into the ground where you want them to grow and can tolerate cold and frosts. Often they can be sown in late autumn or early spring. Talk about low maintenance!

Half-hardy annuals

These are plants that need some more nurturing by planting
in seedling containers under shelter away from frost before
transplanting into their garden position once well established.
Late frost can surprise you, so resist exposing them to the
elements too early.

Below:
*Penstemon
'Garnet' and
Sisyrinchium
striatum* pop
up their heads
behind *Oenothera
lindheimeri* (gaura)
and *Knautia
macedonica.*

BIENNIALS

Unlike annuals, biennials complete their life cycle over two years.
In the first year, they germinate from seed and establish their roots,
stems and leaves; in the second they flower, seed, then die.

Once you get them in a self-seeding cycle they'll be there every year,
and it will seem as though they are flowering annuals with no cost!

Garden equipment
WHEN TO SPLURGE AND WHEN TO SAVE

After years of trial and error, I have finally learned my lesson choosing practical equipment for garden jobs – and knowing when to spend a bit more on quality tools that will last.

At first, the nature of these non-glamorous purchases definitely led me to keep the budget as low as possible, because art, clothing and delicious dinners out are important to me, too!

But repeated experiences of bottom-of-the-rack secateurs disintegrating within a month, 90-degree bends in trowels on the first dig and the tiresome frustration of flaky hose links that dribble or blow off the tap taught me I needed a new approach.

While there are certainly exceptions to the rule, more often than not I have now found that the concept of 'buy once, buy well' has great weight when purchasing for my garden life. After much pushing of the boundaries, only now do I feel that I have a solid collection of garden artillery that is truly going to last the distance and reliably assist me in the way the packaging descriptions promise.

Choosing tools is very much based on the type and size of your plot and on what you want to grow. Many of my own favourite tools have come from personal recommendations so I thought I would share some with those just starting out on this growing adventure in the hope I can help you to avoid wasting money. There are times to save and times to splurge.

SPLURGE ON . . .

1. Handheld hoe

I use the Niwashi brand. It is a traditional Japanese handheld hoe designed to act as an extension of your arm. This is by far my most versatile and handy tool in the garden. Perfect at spiking out weeds, easily parting soil to pop in seedlings or going for the mega-slash on my decaying dahlia stems. There are many other brands that produce this style of tool, as well as right- and left-handed options which can make gardening jobs easier depending on your preference.

2. Quality hose and attachments

I shudder at the summers spent battling it out with a cheapish hose, the temperamental attachments and its iron-clad commitment of no less than fifty kinks per use. If you are a regular, hose-based waterer during summer, then I can wholeheartedly support the splurge on a top-of-the-line, non-kinking (which really means 'less kinking') hose that comes with its own retractable reel.

Your challenge is to find somewhere to mount it near a tap, but that auto-retracting action is honestly the Rolls Royce of garden experiences and so worth it. The cherry on top is a multi-function nozzle that allows you to control the speed and type of flow. Rather than a strong single stream, I find the shower setting is less disruptive to soil. Life-changing.

GARDEN
EQUIPMENT

SPLURGE
ON

Handheld
hoe

Quality
hose and
attachments

Cutting
'quiver'

Hand trowel

Spade
and fork

SAVE ON

Garden
gloves and
face mask

Stakes

8

Garden bag

3. Cutting 'quiver'

You will discover your unique cutting needs as you work through the jobs that your own garden presents you with. I have come to realise that my perfect collection of cutting tools includes a slim-nosed pair of garden snips (with springs) for harvesting and conditioning flowers for the vase and a sturdy, expensive pair of secateurs for all rose pruning and cutting back of perennials.

In addition, I have some hedge shears for tidying up the topiary and a handy little pruning saw for sorting out tree branches. Trust me when I say that I have had multiple goes at purchasing many of these and simply found that scaling up my budget has meant I now have a collection of cutting tools that will last me indefinitely.

4. Hand trowel

In short, I have discovered you truly get what you pay for here. There is nothing more wildly infuriating than your cheapish new trowel buckling at the first bit of force you apply to it – nothing!

5. Spade and fork

This is a true save or splurge fence-sitter. You could trawl secondhand markets for old, solid garden spades and forks which historically were better quality than many options today. These tend to be made of much sturdier stuff. If you are handy, it might be a case of replacing the decaying wooden handle with a new one, easily picked up from most hardware stores (however the actual replacing can be a big challenge in itself).

Alternatively, if buying new, spend as much as you can afford. These truly are items that you can buy once and have forever if you give them a healthy allowance in your garden budget. I have bent a new, low-budget fork on its first dig, which was incredibly frustrating.

Buy once, buy well.

SAVE ON . . .

6. Garden gloves and face mask

I wear garden gloves for ninety per cent of my outside jobs. I have bought low and high on these and have discovered, no matter what, I will wear them out. So, no need to go flash, but trust me when I say they help you get gritty and tough while protecting your hands from spiky plants and sharp roots.

Equally, I diligently wear gloves and a mask when handling any bagged compost or potting mix to protect myself from Legionnaires' disease, which can be found in dry organic material.

Face masks get dirty and lost, so having a backup supply of inexpensive, disposable masks means there is no excuse not to use them. Some people also choose to wear eye protection to limit dangerous spores' access to their body.

7. Stakes

I have swathes of staking options at my disposal now, both cheap and well-made and beautiful. I find this is a case of prioritising your spending and needs as you grow your tool kit.

I have gotten by with entry-level bamboo hoops and stakes very well for years, although having to restock due to their eventual demise is a side effect. This last season I acquired some beautiful iron stakes and plant supports, which both look great and do the job with no scary snapping! The best part is I know that I will own them for life.

The need to stake plants and the cost of buying the materials can be a surprise for new gardeners, but it is inescapable for some plants. Bamboo or wooden stakes combined with sturdy pruned branches from your own trees will do the job for beginners; more permanent options could be purchased in the future.

8. Garden bag

Some of my most commonly used garden companions are a fleet of tough bags that I drag around, filling as I prune and weed. Once full, they are squashed into the back of my car and taken to the green-waste depot.

This is the reality for many urban-based gardeners where large-scale composting space isn't available at home and having a bag that won't leak is a must!

Below: Metal garden stakes might be a splurge but they add a little beauty as well as function and outlast wooden ones.

There are so many options out there on the market, but I always come back to the very basic and simple function that I need this bag to do – which requires it to be tough, have no holes and good stitching around the handles. I have found that the cheaper ones do just as well as the fancy brand name ones.

Botanical plant names
A UNIVERSAL LANGUAGE

Before I started gardening, one of the biggest hurdles stopping me from getting going was wondering how I could possibly remember any plant names. For me, it was right up there with understanding business accounting. Practically impossible.

But like many things in this whole gardening ride, I was surprised by the fact that the common names of plants I started collecting stuck in my mind like drops of sap, underlining the fact that we can learn anything if we have an interest in it! The botanical names, however, were another level of mystery, and one that I initially, and naively, shoved aside as unnecessary. That was, until I went looking for *Verbena bonariensis*.

In the UK, if you want to find *Verbena bonariensis* you can walk into any garden centre, ask for 'verbena' and leave with exactly what you hoped for. I quickly discovered that going through the same process here in New Zealand got me marched to the bedding plants table and presented with the compact annual, garden verbena.

My initial battle to source *Verbena bonariensis* was due to two factors: the plant itself is scarce here; and its regional, common name in the Northern Hemisphere does not match up to the name used in New Zealand.

Learning my lesson, I locked in its botanical name for a local online search, instantly tracked down seed and was on my way, thus demonstrating to myself exactly why botanical names are relevant and important.

The Swedish botanist Carl Linnaeus developed the binomial (two names) system of naming plants in the 1700s. At the time, Latin was the language of science and the binomial system was also used in the study of animals. Botanical names have expanded over time to use both Latin and Greek-derived words.

While Latin can feel distinctly irrelevant to most of us now, as well as somewhat dismissive of regional language and the naming of plants from the lands they are native to, Latin does enable a unified format that allows plants to be identified, discussed and researched cohesively on a global scale.

In our own analysis here, we will start near the top of the botanical nomenclature system, with plant families. These can be fascinating to investigate, as we find scientific links between plant species we know and love.

Each family is then divided into genus, species, botanical variety (wild origin), cultivar (human origin) and hybrid. For example, Verbenaceae is a plant family that includes 32 genera (including our subject family, verbena) and 800 different species with resulting varieties, cultivars and hybrid examples.

The botanical name of a plant, in its simplest form, is made up of two parts. The first is the plant's 'genus' (plural: genera). It's useful to think of this as its 'surname'. This should always be written with a

capital first letter and italicised.

The second part is the 'specific epithet' (an epithet is a Latin adjective). This word applies to the plant's defining characteristics within the genus. This should not have a capital letter but is always italicised.

The combination of these two words is called the 'species name' or 'botanical name'. For example, you can consider *Verbena bonariensis* and *Verbena* x *hybrida* (the garden verbena I mentioned) to be on the same family tree but on different branches of it.

Often, within the species, there are plants that have naturally evolved to be different enough to require a new definition as a unique variety. While they are on the same large branch of the family tree, you could imagine them to be on their own little leafy stem, so to speak.

If this new trait has occurred naturally and continuously appears over time in its offspring, this emerging variety in the family will be indicated by the botanical name, followed by a non-italicised 'var.' and its new given name. Plants grown from this seed will produce 'true to type' to its parent plant. For instance, *Verbena officinalis* var. *grandiflora*.

If the new traits in the plant have emerged as a result of cultivation helped along by humans, this is called a 'cultivar' (cultivated variety). Cultivars can include an unusual form of a species found in the wild, collected and propagated further, an interesting plant that formed by chance in a garden or nursery, or a hybrid.

These days the botanical names for cultivars are simply displayed as the species name concluded with its given name, non-italicised with a capital, sitting between single quotation marks. For example, *Verbena bonariensis* 'Lollipop'. While it's not theoretically correct, the terms variety and cultivar are often used interchangeably.

Lastly, there is the hybrid, and this is where the botanical names get

Opposite:
Structural stems
of *Verbena
bonariensis*.

BOTANICAL
NAMES
EXPLAINED

In most simple terms useful for home gardeners.

FAMILY

GENERA
Think of as a plant's surname.
Italicised with a capital first letter.

SPECIES
Identifying features of a plant.
Always italicised and in lower case.

GENUS (Genera)	**+**	SPECIFIC EPITHET (Species)	**=**	BOTANICAL PLANT NAME

VARIETY
Occurs in nature.
Italicised and preceded by var.

CULTIVAR
Cultivated by humans.
Non-italicised with a capital first letter
and single quotation marks.

Example using rudbeckia

FAMILY
Asteraceae

GENERA
Rudbeckia

SPECIES
As described by botanical plant name and indication of
variety or cultivar (20+ different species)

—— example ——   —— example ——

Rudbeckia fulgida var.
deamii

Rudbeckia nitida
'Herbstsonne'

a little more complicated.

Keeping it light, a hybrid is a result of crossing two different species or varieties that can both occur naturally or through human experimentation. The results include characteristics of both plants, and seeds saved from hybrids don't result in plants 'true to type'. Division or cuttings would be needed to grow another plant in its exact image.

Sometimes these plants are indicated by the parent species' genus separated by an non-italicised 'x' followed by the new name for the resulting cross, which can often simply be '*hybrida*' as seen with *Verbena* x *hybrida*. Other times, it might be the two parent species' names separated by 'x'. Confusingly, hybrids helped along by humans are also cultivars.

Deep breath!

As you explore botanical names you start to see that the specific epithet will often give clues about the plant, even if you haven't seen it before. Sometimes it can be a Greek-inspired version of the person who introduced it into the nomenclature system. For example, our native grass *Carex buchananii* is named after early New Zealand botanist John Buchanan.

Other times, recognisable Latin can hint at the plant's characteristics, such as *alba* indicating white, *purpurea* purple and *rubra* red.

And, as you become familiar with this system, you will soon recognise reoccurring specific epithets that you can relate to other plants you know. Like *hastata* suggesting spear-shaped, *echinops* being spikey and *latifolius*, broad-leaved.

You don't need a science degree to grasp a basic knowledge of botanical names and knowing plants beyond their common names unlocks the potential of your future planting and sourcing.

Previous page: *Echinacea purpurea* 'Alba' with *Sanguisorba officinalis*. **Opposite:** *Echinacea purpurea, Rudbeckia hirta* 'Irish Eyes' with dots of *Sanguisorba officinalis* and the bright red of *Geum chiloense* 'Mrs Bradshaw'.

Pollination

IT MAKEʃ THE WORLD GO ROUND

Thanks to the basic botany taught in classrooms everywhere, as a child I could confidently identify the anthers, stamens and reproductive workings of a flower, including a simplistic description of the process of pollination. It was practically a rite of passage for primary school students in New Zealand. To be fair, much of that information was later smothered by less important but consuming knowledge needed for adulthood and it wasn't until I started gardening that it bubbled back to the surface.

With my rediscovery of the natural world and her processes through the making of my own garden in my mid-thirties, I've enjoyed observing the increased movement of bees around my beds, knowing that this is indeed a good thing. On occasion, I have even felt the need to justify my focus on flower gardening (as opposed to food growing) by finishing descriptions of my garden with 'Of course, I grow flowers for the pollinators . . . you know.'

If nothing else, the fact that one in three mouthfuls of food we eat is the result of animal pollination drives home our reliance on such beasts,

Opposite: Bumblebees flocking to *Echinacea purpurea* 'Alba' with spikes of *Veronica longifolia* 'Alba.'

and flower-growing supports their sustenance!

To drag you back to your classroom roots, the process of pollination is described as the transferal of a plant's pollen (male genetic material) from the anther (part of the stamen, which is the male anatomy of a flower) to the stigma (part of the pistil, which is the female anatomy of the flower). The result is fertilisation and the ability of a plant to create fruit and/or seeds to continue its species' survival.

Yes, this is botanical sex, but with a helpful third party – the pollinator.

The transfer of pollen can be aided by wind and water or by insects and mammals. Plants have evolved in a way that ensures the ongoing diversification and health of their own species, designing themselves to appeal specifically to the pollinator that best suits their conditions and needs. Their fragrance, colour, shape and even flowering time are directly marketing to the preferences of their chosen pollinator, who is on the lookout for sources of delicious nectar and nutritious pollen. We are just the lucky bystanders that admire and sometimes host the activity.

Most plants prefer to be pollinated with pollen from another of their own species, which is called 'cross-pollination'.

A flower's fertilisation from either its own pollen or that from another flower on the same plant can result in poor seed production and less vigorous seedlings. This is called 'selfing', and is essentially inbreeding. At times it is hard for the plant to avoid this.

Some plants, such as tomatoes, try to reduce 'selfing' by ripening their anther a few weeks before their stigma. This plant would be considered 'complete' as it has both male and female elements in a single flower, categorizing it as 'bisexual'.

Plants like most cucurbits and corn are considered to be 'monoecious', producing separate male and female flowers on the same plant, sometimes at different times, which is considered 'unisexual'. In addition, plants like kiwifruit, cannabis and many trees produce only male or only female parts on entirely separate specimens. These are referred to as 'dioecious', and when used in public planting, male trees are often chosen to avoid the mess of flowers and fruit. The flip side is that there will be a high density of pollen, which makes life tricky for those with hay fever!

Effective pollination is made much easier if we take into account the habits of some of our most common pollinators. For instance, each separate foraging trip that a honeybee makes is focused on a single plant type (this was news to me!). News of good nectar and pollen sources is shared between bees in the form of the 'waggle dance'. A bee will waggle and turn its body to describe the distance, direction and type of plant that its fellow foragers should explore.

These trips will involve visiting between fifty and one hundred flowers on their mission to collect pollen, loaded with essential nutrients for young bee larvae, while concurrently feasting on nectar for their own energy reserves. While most pollen is stored neatly into their leg pouches for home delivery, their busy, industrious activity results in their hairy bodies being coated with excess pollen too. This is subsequently dragged and dropped across stigmas, completing the process desired by plants!

In contrast, I was intrigued to find that bumblebees provide a similar but turbo-boosted service that is desirable for many plants, including tomatoes, blueberries and eggplants amongst others. These plants don't give up their pollen quite as easily and require a close-contact vibration frequency to release it. This is called 'buzz pollination' (or sonication), and this is where the bumble bee reigns supreme! Listen closely for that furious bumblebee buzzing next time you're in the garden.

While exploring this busy garden-based industry, I took myself outside to observe my own pollinator crew in action. I spent an hour with my nose at bloom level, using my eyes, my camera and the slow-mo video setting on my phone for close observation. It was truly fascinating and I marveled at the challenges faced by each pollinator as they navigated the vast diversity in flower architecture. By far and wide the plants receiving the most attention in the garden, including regular clashes on arrival between the bossy bumble bees and nippy bees, were the single-petal dahlias, the echinacea and the helenium. My sanguisorba crop, with its dense flower heads, didn't seem popular at all, which I felt was understandable!

What's more, for the first time, I noticed the occasional metallic green soldier fly quietly picking over my astrantia and eryngium, approaching their work with a little less gusto than their busier, larger competition. It hadn't really dawned on me that flies, along with butterflies and moths, are also important contributors to the pollination circus.

I encourage you to take some time out and see who the pollinators are in your own garden. It's a busy, productive and beautiful workplace to look in on.

Below: Monarch butterflies flock to *Verbena bonariensis.*

I encourage you to take some time out and see who the pollinators are in your own garden. It's a busy, productive and beautiful workplace to look in on.

A VISIT TO...

Flaxme garden

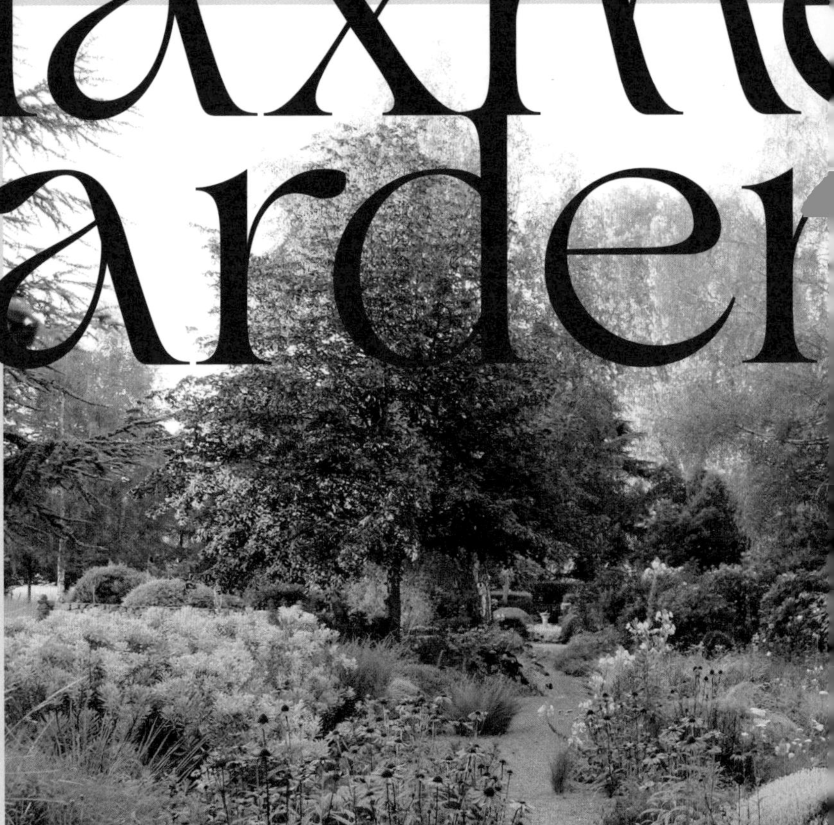

The magical naturalistic planting at Flaxmere garden under a summer's dawn.

WITH PENNY ZINO

ere

Into the realm...

I first visited Penny Zino's garden Flaxmere in 2017 when my passion for gardening was only in its fledgling state. I had driven there for a sculpture exhibition, but my pale green thumbs had just enough influence over me to start examining the environment the art sat in.

That initial experience, and the many following at Flaxmere, opened my eyes to gardens as 'spaces' rather than just places. Any preconceived ideas I had about them being delicate or quaint were rapidly unravelled. Flaxmere was a realm.

Oaks, redwoods, eucalypts, beech, poplars and other giant creatures I can't name stand protectively over visitors to the garden. They seem to step sideways to usher you down secret leafy paths, channelling you to one of many bridges to dramatically reveal the view of Mt Tekoa. This isn't a singular space, but many that are artfully linked together, transitioning you to distinctly different atmospheres as you explore. As a 6-star Garden of International Significance, Flaxmere is a fascinating place that kick-started my appreciation of the power of planting.

Opposite: Gardener Penny Zino put a wind-felled eucalyptus to creative use by fashioning a silvery whirlpool with its limbs, interplanting with *Carex comans* 'Green' tussock.

For over half a century, Penny has conjured her garden-scapes into existence on top of 3.5 hectares of farmland. Bordered by the steep foothills of the Southern Alps, a braided river and flats that the nor'west wind loves to rip across, it certainly couldn't be claimed to be a friendly growing zone. Unseasonal snow and frosts, droughts and livestock break-ins all come part and parcel with the location, causing great frustration and often, great devastation of Flaxmere's plant population!

The outcome of Penny's creation of such an expansive garden over decades is that you witness her progression in tastes and horticultural interests. Pooling between trees are spaces with beautiful, site-specific planting flowing out into the larger areas of light. Within the landscape, there are 'rooms' focusing on woodland, water's edge and native planting. Sumptuous rhododendrons and azaleas sprinkle colour during springtime, while huge clipped topiary balls march you down to the pool area and adjacent rose garden. You'll even pass a striking 'whirlpool' of grasses swirling within a driftwood ring before you pick your way along the hidden pond path in the company of Mrs Swan and friends. Extensive stone walls border areas of the garden, made laboriously by hand by Penny herself, nodding at her unrivalled drive to reach her vision.

This is a garden for the seasons, a moving ode to Mother Nature's annual cycle. A plant person would feast in this place, a beginner will find the fire to learn more.

The world of garden design, just like any other, ebbs and flows with changing times and perspectives on putting spaces together. Penny has not been one to stand idle on the edges and watch this happen. In 2012 she and great friend and fellow gardener, Robyn Kilty (page 128), flew to the Netherlands to attend a workshop with world-renowned designer Piet Oudolf.

Above: Giant buxus balls guide garden explorers down to the pool. **Below:** Shady pathways criss-cross the expansive garden.

Above: Backlit by the dawn glow, *Persicaria amplexicaulis* 'Firetail', *Echinacea purpurea* and the feathery wands of *Stipa gigantea* fuel the wild beauty of this planting. **Right:** Penny started her rural 3.5 hectare garden from scratch 56 years ago and continues to develop it today.

Flaxmere is Penny's paint palette which she can mix, shift and apply differently as a way to flex her curiosity and creativity, no matter the season.

The women were fascinated by his take on the New Perennial Movement, mixing perennials with textural grasses to achieve a curated but soft, naturalistic look (page 174). This whimsical, borderless planting based on changing palettes and form throughout the seasons was in huge contrast to the structured, somewhat traditional ideals of the New Zealand gardens popular in the decades since its colonisation.

Penny returned home with a plan of attack and, over just a few years, the result is a truly magical area of Flaxmere that is under constant review and tweaking as she tailors this concept to her harsh environment. For those, like me, who are really attracted to this style of planting, it is an incredible treat to be able to visit this large homegrown example throughout the seasons.

Wandering the garden with Penny I am constantly reminded that creating spaces and working with plants has no endpoint. I listen intently as she tells me about all the new challenges that have cropped up in this landscape, which trees need to come out, and her valuable snippets about what is and isn't working in her naturalistic garden.

To put some context around this, not many people get to discuss the eventual need to remove trees they planted due to their size and instability! By beginning her planting in 1967, Penny has essentially witnessed the full maturity and in some cases, the eventual demise of her earlier vision, something that I won't get to see myself on the same scale due to my starting out later in life.

But more than anything, I listen to her new ideas, changing plans and the unending passion that it all rests on. She is a prime example of the advantages of being an observer, allowing former ideals to be replaced as knowledge and experience builds through trial and error. Flaxmere is Penny's paint palette, which she can mix, shift and apply differently as a way to flex her curiosity and creativity, no matter the season.

Opposite: A stream runs through the garden, pooling in places as a pond rich with bird and aquatic life.

Collecting seed
THE MAGIC AND THE MESS

Each autumn as I watch my flower garden melt away for the winter in all its blotchy, yellowing, mildewy glory, I find it hard to ignore the fuzzy, graphic balls floating above the leafy mess.

For first-time gardeners, it's easy to miss the gold to be found at this time of year when you lament that your lovely outside space isn't actually static. This is our 'lesson' time after the main show of the blooms, and a reminder that you are working within a moving medium that waits for no one.

Seedheads are fascinating things – all architectural and intricate in their design, with the sole aim of the survival of their species. They literally want to 'spread their seed' and ensure their legacy of future plant babies from their family line. It's mind-blowing when you think about the science of it all.

Opposite above: The fading blooms of cosmos sinking into seed. **Opposite below:** Cracking open a nigella seedhead.

Seeds are also a currency for gardeners. Envelopes of seed are traded in return for others, sold, stored, germinated undercover or just flung at the soil with fingers crossed. Growing your own flowers

Seedheads are fascinating things - all architectural and intricate in their design, with the sole aim of the survival of their species.

equals the opportunity to grow even more in the future at no cost – just a little effort and forward planning.

I am the first to admit that I find the process of preparing seed trays, sowing and pampering seedlings to success a little laborious, but it was my first purchase of seed that showed me the huge creative potential of curating a garden, igniting a thirst to hunt out and grow the weird and the wonderful.

I've learned to be patient and let the seedheads dry out on the plant, testing their ripeness by running my thumb lightly over their heads. If the seeds pull out easily, I then snip off the whole head and pop it into an envelope to process later. Sometimes much, much later! I have piles of envelopes with collected seed that I have never done anything with, but couldn't bear to let 'go to waste'. Fresh seed has a much better chance of germination than old seed, so it's best not to store it for years.

Like all the books say, seed needs to be stored in a dry environment, which is why breathable paper bags are a good option. As first-timers you will discover that the seedheads you collect aren't simply made up of the precious seeds themselves; they are also full of flaky, protective husks (referred to as chaff), which can add confusion.

Separating the seed from the chaff isn't my favourite task either, but I did stumble upon an efficient old technique called winnowing. This is a process based on the fact that lighter substances will blow away before heavier ones, and in this case, seeds are heavier than husks.

Use your fingers to break down the seedheads into a shallow bowl and very gently blow into your seed 'material'. Like magic, the lightweight husks float up and away, leaving a well-sorted pile of seed at the bottom of the bowl, ready to use as you wish. This might not be an effective method for large-scale seed collectors, but for home gardeners, it's a pretty basic and easy option.

Growing from seed

A PARTNERSHIP WITH MOTHER NATURE

Even if you haven't grown anything since those potato heads in primary school, you are in luck – ultimately, seeds want to grow. So with Mother Nature on your side, and a gentle reminder that it's very common for seeds not to germinate, too, below is a guide to how I get them going.

MY BEGINNER'S KIT FOR STARTING SEEDS

Seed mix

You can buy this from garden centres or hardware stores. Essentially it is newborn plant-friendly potting mix with all the right healthy bits and nothing too strong.

Propagator

This sounds serious, but it's not! I have one that I use over and over as it is essentially a mini greenhouse. The little cells sit on a bio fabric that sucks water through to the bases of each cell. It also has a

Opposite:
Crispy
seedheads
of fennel.

clear plastic lid to keep things humid and cosy. It is robust and I use it year after year. I find using a propagator helps avoid overwatering my seedlings.

Modular seed trays

You can use these instead of a propagator. Reusing punnets from the garden centre or even egg cartons will work, too! These will need to sit in a tray that you can top up with water, allowing them to suck up the moisture from the bottom of the cells. Simply use a clear plastic bag over the top to imitate the humid conditions of the propagator during germination.

Another alternative to a propagator are biodegradable seed cells. These are quite good for larger seeds that are sturdy. As they emerge through the soil and after forming a few sets of leaves, they can be planted out into the garden complete with the pot, which will break down.

Larger reusable pots

You can use these to graduate your baby seedlings into before planting out in the garden. This is commonly referred to as 'potting on'. I always save the plastic punnets I receive when buying plants from the garden centre and reuse them in this way.

Gardening gloves and face mask for handling dry seed mix

Legionnaire's disease can be contracted by inhaling or spreading the bacteria from hand to mouth when handling dry bagged potting mix or compost.

Trays

For resting seed cells/punnets in to sap up water from their bases.

I have used old roasting trays for this many a time as they are easy to top up from the edges and, if flat, allow water to be evenly distributed.

SEED SIZE

Before you begin, consider the size of your seed. Teeny seeds that look like dust are best sprinkled lightly on the surface of your seed mix-filled punnets. Spray a little water on them to get them started, and sit the punnets in a tray of water, or use a propagator for perfect water delivery.

It is possible to keep them too wet, too! So just monitor them daily, treating them like your babies.

Bigger seeds like sweet peas can be planted one at a time and pushed deeper into the seed mix in the punnet. Use a pencil or something similar to punch a little hole, then drop the seed into it and gently cover over. Erin Benzakein sums it up best in her book *Cut Flower Garden*: 'A general rule of thumb is to plant the seed twice as deep as its longest side.'

POSITIONING AND CARE

After you have filled your trays/punnets/pottles/pots with seed mix and then dressed them with their seeds, you need to offer them a very friendly environment to germinate. During the germination stage they like gentle warmth and moisture to get their first shoots to pop through the soil. A sheltered bright spot like a back porch, windowsill or even kitchen table can work.

Humidity is helpful, too, and can be achieved by using the clear lid of your propagator or even a loosely draped plastic bag. Once it gets warmer and your seedlings are growing, leave off the lid or cover during the day to promote airflow, returning them to cosy in the evenings.

Propagators have a water delivery system that is easily topped up and delivers an ideal amount of water to your seedling cells. Alternatively, if using seedling punnets, they need to be seated in a tray topped up with water so they can hydrate from their bases, avoiding the risk of washing seeds away by watering from the top. Daily checks are needed so your punnets don't dry out. Equally, you want to avoid having them sitting in water full-time as this will deliver nasty problems like mildew and seedling death/non-germination. Overwatered seedlings may recover on their own if you let them dry out a little, providing their roots haven't rotted. It's a juggle that just requires regular checks.

Once my seedlings get a couple of sets of leaves, I then leave any covers off and they naturally harden off with the fluctuations in heat during the day in their covered outdoor position. Keeping them covered for too long will make them spindly as they grow in their luxurious warm home, unprepared for life in the garden.

POTTING ON AND GRADUATING TO THE GARDEN

To make room in my propagator for more seeds, once they have their first set of leaves that resemble their parent plant, I graduate my seedlings by gently 'pricking them out' of their seedling mix using a chopstick or similar. Use the stick to lightly support the base of the seedling while carefully pulling it up through the mix. I then replant them into larger pots in small groups, leaving them with room to mature. This is called 'potting on'. I generally fill their new home with potting mix as opposed to other options.

Opposite above: Harvesting *Rudbeckia fulgida* var. *deamii* seedheads.
Opposite below: Saving an echinacea seedhead.

In terms of moving the new plants to the garden, I took inspiration when I first started gardening from the size of the smaller seedlings in trays that I would buy at the garden centre. Once mine appear a similar size and seem healthy, off they go!

At this stage, they will have three to four sets of leaves.

Once in the wild of your garden, your little plants will have a target on their back for birds looking to have an aggressive scratch around in the newly disturbed soil around them.

I combat this by building a small twig fortress around the most exposed ones to protect them, however net or wire netting tunnels would be less labour intensive!

Be sure to research the ideal growing conditions for your plant that you have brought to life. Don't waste all your early effort and care by homing your plant in a shady position in the garden when it requires full sun to be the best plant it can be.

And importantly, don't worry if you have some failures – they are guaranteed in gardening!

SOWING DIRECT INTO THE GARDEN

Can your seeds be planted direct in the ground where you would like them to grow? Read your seed packet, note from seller, or look for information online. Some plants don't like to be moved from pot to ground, so it's important to understand the needs of what you are planting.

If this is the case and your seed likes to be planted directly into the earth, just wait until the ground warms up a bit in mid to late spring. Look for the arrival of annual weeds starting to green up the bare parts of your garden – this is a good sign that the ground is warm enough and ready.

Opposite above: An optional layer of vermiculite can be sprinkled over seedling cells to assist in water and nutrient retention. **Opposite below:** Seedlings in a cosy bright spot.

You can sow seeds any time through to late spring/early summer; after that I'd suggest purchasing already established seedlings to plug into the garden to give you a chance for some colour before the frosts. Also, be sure to mark the location of your seed so you know not to weed it out.

Restocking your garden beds

HOW TO TAKE CUTTINGS AND DIVIDE PERENNIALS

Unlock the money-saving potential of your planting by investigating which specimens you can easily multiply. With a little research you will be able to identify which plants you can take cuttings from and which you could dig up and divide. These options are a pathway to a full garden without further spend.

WHAT IS A CUTTING?

To take a 'cutting' is to remove a section of a parent plant – be it a stem, leaf or root – to produce another of the exact same type by giving it suitable conditions to root, grow and flourish. Not all plants can be grown from a cutting and different plants favour different methods.

As a base rule, growing from cuttings is best done with shrubs, perennials and vines. Annuals, with their rapid life cycle, are mostly not good options.

WHEN TO TAKE CUTTINGS

It's possible to identify suitable stems and take cuttings from late spring into early winter and it is most definitely worth researching your target plants to identify their best time.

You want to avoid the immaturity of very young, new shoots in early spring and instead wait a little longer to take soft-wood cuttings. You can test the stage your plant is at by bending a stem in half. If it breaks (instead of just springing back into shape) it is now in the excellent soft-wood stage.

For soft-wood cuttings, snip vibrant new growth in late spring to early summer. In summer you can take 'semi-ripe' cuttings where the stem you select has hardened a little further but the tips are still fresh and supple. Hardwood cuttings of matured woody stems can be taken from autumn into early winter in the plant's dormancy.

Opposite: A small prepared cutting.

From here I will concentrate on the process for soft-wood/semi-ripe cuttings. Hardwood cuttings have some minor differences and are done as the plant sinks into dormancy.

HOW TO TAKE A SOFT-WOOD CUTTING

Before you make your cutting, you need to prepare its growing medium. Fill a pot or tray with propagating mix (often called cutting mix) for best results. Some people use grainy sand or make their own mixes, but unlike regular potting mix, it is important that this medium is light and free draining. It is easy to pick up a small bag from the garden centre. The next step is to thoroughly soak it through with water.

The basic method of making a cutting is the same for most plants, no matter the maturity of the selected stem.

When making a selection, identify a stem of this season's new growth (rather than hardened wood from previous years) that has not produced buds or flowers. These may be smaller side shoots down the main stem or body of the plant.

First thing in the morning, when the plant is hydrated, select a stem from a disease-free, vigorous plant for best results. With a sharp, clean pair of secateurs or a knife, measure 7–10cm down from the tip, making your cut just below a leaf joint (commonly referred to as a node). This is where your new roots will bud from.

Strip off those leaves you have cut just below and any others on the lower third of the cutting. If your plant has broad leaves, snip the remaining leaves in half, leaving the little or slim ones whole. Your cutting is now vulnerable with no roots, so reducing the leaf area will relieve its strain but still allow it surface area to photosynthesise and grow.

You then have the option to dip the heel of your cutting into a rooting hormone, easily purchased from a garden centre. This is supposed to invigorate the growth of roots and keep any harmful bacteria at bay, but many wise gardeners I know skip this step. Perhaps it is most helpful for woodier stems.

Gently force your cutting into your lightly tamped down, level propagating mix until the lowest set of leaves is just above the surface, and firm down the mix around it. You want enough stem in the ground to have a supportive base for your establishing plant. It can be a good idea to plant your cuttings around the inner edges of a pot to aid in support. You can plant multiple cuttings in a single pot!

HOW TO CARE FOR YOUR CUTTINGS

To care for your plant babies, soil needs to be kept moist but not damp. A misting spray bottle can come in handy and so can a plastic bag over the pot, which will both allow light in and create delicious humidity. Remove the bag a few times a week to allow for ventilation. Position cuttings out of direct sunlight, particularly in the hot summer months.

Fresh cuttings can look a little sad for a few weeks, and, depending on the plant variety, can take 4–10 weeks to root. Gently tug at your specimens to see if there is any resistance indicating roots, or watch for the telltale signs of new leaf growth showing success!

Once rooted, you can transfer the plant to a larger pot on its own (no plastic bag needed), where it will be ready for planting out in about a month or when the weather warms up again.

HOW TO TAKE A HARDWOOD CUTTING

The process is largely the same as above and used for deciduous shrubs and trees with woody stems compared to those used for semi-ripe/soft-wood cuttings.

Look for stems of this season's growth that are about a pencil's thickness. Remove them with a horizontal cut below a leaf node or bud. Measure your cut stem to 15cm or so, trimming a section off just above a node or bud. You may be able to create several cuttings from one removed stem.

Plant your cuttings (with or without rooting compound) into your pot of cutting mix to a depth of around 10cm. Multiple cuttings can be planted in the same pot.

Hardwood cuttings can take much longer to form roots. Keep your potted cuttings undercover but not heated, watering when necessary and leave for a year, or until roots appear out the bottom, before planting out into the garden.

HOW TO DIVIDE

Dividing plants often requires some muscle, and never quite looks like it does in the books, but it is a remarkably easy way to increase the population of your favourite plants in the garden. Cheap (or free!), too.

Division of your perennials is best done in autumn or spring. Dig up your plant using a spade or garden fork. Give the plant a bit of a shake to remove clumps of dirt, which allows you a clear view of its shape. Use a hose to remove soil if you like.

Sometimes you can prise the roots apart and make divisions simply using your hands. If not, use a sharp spade to slice through the clump.

You may continue to divide a few times, however, err on the side of caution to ensure you have good healthy root stock in each section.

Replant your divisions, water and hope for the best!

To take a
'cutting' is to
remove a section
of a parent plant
- be it a stem,
leaf or root - to
produce another
of the exact
type by giving
it favourable
conditions to
root, grow and
flourish.

Garden centre shopping

KICKSTART YOUR PERENNIAL PLANTING

When summer turns to autumn, we gardeners are rewarded with the fantastic arrival of garden centre sales. This is most exciting for those of us who are into flowering perennials (page 214), which bring our spaces so much seasonal interest and joy.

Autumn is a terrific time to go wander the aisles (or do so virtually with your favourite online nurseries) and see if you might just stumble across a deal or two. Perennials are already great investments in that after a year or two, you can dig up the mature clumps, divide them into 'new' plants with a sharp spade and replant, drastically multiplying your garden stock (page 70).

I like to think of flowering perennials as the delicious, slowly unveiling 'decoration' of my garden. They even 'put themselves away' with minimal help and a quick chop each winter. They are your garden's party earrings – or the lipstick that it puts on to feel great on a gloomy day – and your own offering to Mother Nature's bees, moths and butterflies.

Opposite: Planting out perennials purchased from the garden centre in autumn.

One of the biggest adjustments I have had to make is letting go of instant gratification and understanding that planting perennials in autumn (which will be dormant over winter) will aid my garden but results might not be seen for six months or more. What follows is a guide to help you make the most of garden centre sales and choosing plants you prefer.

YOUR GARDEN, YOUR STYLE

Choosing plants can be quite overwhelming, whether it be your first time starting from scratch or working to transform your current garden into one that personally makes your heart sing.

I have learnt (after my beginnings of buying *one* of every plant that attracted me, like a magpie) that curating beds by repeating plants of fewer varieties gives a really rich and luxurious feeling.

You might prefer a limited soft palette or brave colour chaos, but don't forget to consider the mix of texture versus shape of bloom versus foliage and of course, a plant's water and sun needs in relation to the environment you are working in. Finding variation in flower and plant size will give you a beautiful painterly effect (page 214). The cherry on the top here is educating yourself on when each plant you are interested in flowers, enabling you to pair it with others that can take the bloom baton once it is finished.

Another consideration to add to the mix is the way the plants you choose affect the ecosystem of your garden. Efforts to offer nectar then seedheads and fruit for as much of the year as possible will support the insects and animals that call your space home. So continue to investigate the plants you are interested in (the internet is very helpful for this!), make shopping lists, and look for gaps to fill in your seasonal show, connecting your visual needs to the needs of your garden residents.

THINGS TO CONSIDER WHEN SELECTING PERENNIALS

When visiting the garden centre, these simple pointers will help you to focus your search, avoiding coming away with a random assortment of plants that might fight with those you already have in your garden, or dislike the position you have available.

Read the height that each plant is expected to mature to so you can imagine how all these new plants might work together or where they can slot into your existing garden bed.

Pay close attention to how much sun a plant needs. I have in the past (and admittedly I continually push the limits) planted sun-lovers in shade and acted surprised when they didn't grow at all or grew horizontal to the ground, searching for light. A 'full sun' label refers to six hours of sun exposure a day!

The plant you are considering at the garden centre might be flowering but looking a bit sad. Don't worry! It is simply approaching the end of its season before it puts itself to bed for the winter. This is exactly what summer flowering perennials do. This means you are unlikely to get much pleasure from it this year but even if it looks like it has died once it has been planted out, it is most likely receding into dormancy where it will grow its root base, ready for next year.

You don't have to know your purchased plant's final destination in the garden. You can plant it anywhere – ideally, in the position it prefers in regard to sunlight – then dig it up and move it in spring when you can see the gaps better. Perennials are particularly easygoing in this way!

Putting your garden to bed

FOR THE WINTER MONTHS AHEAD

One sticking point for me, as I ventured into growing a seasonal flower garden, was wondering what the books actually meant when they talked about 'putting the garden to bed for winter'? It sure had a delicious, cosy ring to it, but beyond weeding, preparing the garden for the cold months was a bit of a mysterious concept. It's not that I hadn't noticed the beds of tired seedheads and blotchy leaves waving at me, I just felt extremely intimidated by what I was meant to do about them, and when.

Bearing in mind that the different regions of New Zealand vary from subtropical to starkly chilly during the autumn months, your garden will mostly give you its own signs that bedtime might be close.

In the south, the first frosts really speed up the decline of annuals and perennials – evidenced by their droopy, soggy or blackened foliage and the distinct lack of new flowers. Equally, even in warmer climates, some flowering plants will naturally start to die while others begin shooting new growth from their base only.

This general bedraggled vibe signals that your perennials are

Opposite: A busy scene at home as I tidy up my vegetable garden in autumn.

preparing for dormancy and your annuals are giving up the ghost.

Since those early days, I have discovered that pre-winter prep essentially covers a checklist of autumn planting and dividing, snipping, weeding, feeding and mulching. It's the big effort before a somewhat chilled-out few months in the garden. It also isn't an exact science and I have found, thanks to my lack of experience, that chopping back too hard/too early/too late hasn't resulted in any dire circumstances. Lucky for us, our gardens want to go to bed, and are keen to get up again in springtime even if we get the following jobs a little wrong.

Firstly, scoot around and do a solid weed, giving your topiary or evergreen shrubs a wee haircut at the same time to get them tidy for winter, when they'll produce little growth.

Armed with secateurs, snip decaying stalks from perennials that are looking sad rather than architectural. I like to chop them down to stalks of about 20cm, so that I can see and avoid their clumps when adding a layer of mulch. When pruning back you may notice some short fresh growth; some perennials display this, and others will go on to recede completely out of sight, underground. If in doubt, a quick search online will give you specific care information for your individual plant species. If you are getting to know your garden, plunge a labelled stick in the ground nearby so that you remember who lives there even when you can't see them.

You might also choose to leave the strong sculptural frames of some flowering perennials and grasses to provide snacks for birds, chopping back to new low growth or around 20cm in mid to late winter. I often leave herbaceous phlomis, perennial grasses, *Verbena bonariensis*, rudbeckia, echinacea and Japanese anemone seedheads on the plant for longer as they do offer some visual interest.

Rather than completely pulling out limp-looking annuals, they can instead be chopped off at the base, leaving the rotting roots in the ground to contribute excellent organic matter to your soil. Also consider leaving the plants to stand a little longer if you are keen for their ripe seeds to drop freely to encourage a fresh, self-sown crop next year. This is up to you.

The same could be said for your enthusiastic perennials that you know will take over if their seeds reach the ground. Now would be the time to snip those stalks off if you want to avoid this – I do this with my fennel.

This is also a great time to dig up the clumps of your perennials, drive a sharp spade through them and divide them to replant as multiple new plants – a favourite activity of mine for the abundant rewards in the following growing season (page 74).

Next you need to 'pull up the blanket', so to speak, by feeding your soil and adding a layer of mulch to insulate over winter, keeping plants, worms and their microbe friends happy. This also helps to suppress eager weeds!

You may choose to feed your beds before bedtime with homemade compost, or perhaps purchase it in bags – or by the trailer load! Whatever you can afford or have the time and means to get. Aged horse manure, sheep or chicken pellets, blood and bone or all-in-one locally produced bagged products will all benefit the continued health of your garden.

There is no need to get too physical here, just sprinkle over a layer of about 5cm, then gently fork it into the top of the soil, leaving some breathing room around the base of stems or trunks to avoid any chance of rotting. This will be naturally absorbed over the winter months, leaving your garden beds refreshed.

While I don't necessarily 'feed' my ornamental beds each year, the vege garden does tend to get extra attention. Often, a nice layer of biodegradable mulch is enough to work its way in and do a similar job.

Finally, an overall topping of mulch will seal in all your good work. Natural, organic matter is best here with options like wood chip, pea straw, grass clippings or shredded leaves. If you don't have a leaf blower (I know the strong opinions on them!) that can suck up and shred leaves, you can also spread them across the lawn and mow over top, raking up the remains. A nice chunky layer will slowly be absorbed into your garden over time, acting as a conditioner and helping to loosen up soil going forward.

My personal preference for mulching my urban garden is bales of pea straw, which are easy to handle, and any unused can be covered and stashed for a spring top-up.

I think this 'putting to bed' business is the 'work' that non-gardeners fear in creating a seasonal garden. But it's well worth it – a few sessions of huffing and puffing in the crisp autumn air results in the deep satisfaction of a tidied-up plot. Even better are the months of results to be enjoyed over spring, summer and the following autumn.

The reward truly outweighs the work.

Below: A thick layer of pea straw mulch covering freshly created beds. **Next page:** Giant sunflower seedheads versus human.

This 'putting to bed' business is the 'work' that non-gardeners fear in creating a seasonal garden. But it's well worth it - a few sessions of huffing and puffing in the crisp autumn air results in the deep satisfaction of a tidied-up plot.

Structure
in the garden
CREATING JUXTAPOSITION

As a beginner, I initially viewed gardens as a whole. I'd take in the big picture, which either felt appealing or not. It was only by visiting gardens throughout the seasons that I began to see past my favourite bits (the soft, floaty and floral) and appreciate the grounding features that prevented the planting from reading as a Liberty print!

It slowly dawned on me that a garden struggles to take its viewer on a journey without the helping hand of structural elements – strong, solid accents that anchor the seasonal plants to a space and offer us visual pleasure even when the floral and soft have gone to bed for the winter.

The structural elements of a garden could be considered its bones. Manufactured pieces like paved or dressed pathways, raised planters, solid bed edging, trellis, arches, fences or pots, or natural features like hedging, topiary and trees – these are the constants of an outdoor space, the bedrock essentials that exist all year round. During the growing seasons, many might disappear into the background – think rose-smothered arches or topiary balls dotted in perennial planting – only to become the stars of the show in the winter months.

When I recall our inherited garden on the first day we moved into our home, it was mostly about structure. With little perennial planting, the previous owners had focused on strong evergreen options that were mostly static year-round, with very few seasonal surprises. With an inexperienced hand I removed much of this, and in hindsight, I think it was only luck that I didn't squander all of the slower-growing plants that have proven vital in the overall experience of my garden now!

As I have flooded every inch I can with my collected perennials, I have also found myself adding strength back in, too. The raised brick planter at the end of the lawn was built to capture the sun and retain a new bed for planting. Most recently we have not only added a second raised planter but also newly expanded beds edged in brick, using this subtle material to lead the eye through from the brick-paved back porch

Opposite & next page: My new brick retained beds have transformed the lawn into a feature of the garden.

and connect all parts of the garden. Brick was a natural choice given my husband is a bricklayer, but its repetition is intended. By keeping introduced materials to a simple few and repeating their use, I've been able to create a visual story that threads through this little space.

When considering structure in my garden now, I find much of my focus is around juxtaposition. Hard versus soft, smooth versus textural, uniform versus organic. When my garden is in full bloom, the solid elements of the fence and raised beds create separation for the somewhat wild planting.

The simple wooden fence topped with trellis is stained dark, drawing attention down from my neighbours' roofs and providing a dramatic backdrop through the seasons – highlighting glossy greens, floral colour, fiery autumn leaves and wispy seedheads. Had the fence remained natural in tone, the drama would most certainly be missing, as would the sense of dimension.

The value of a lawn as a structural element could probably be argued, but with a few tweaks to its shape, I believe it has transformed how my space is both viewed and experienced. Initially, all beds were mapped out around the edges of the yard, with traditional straight lines and a fairly standard balance of lawn outweighing garden. However, with our recent changes of reclaiming lawn by expanding beds and defining them with swooping strong edges, the remaining grassy space now has a sense of flow. Its soft curve pulls you off into the garden, where it pools in a wider space under the cherry tree before circling off around the central raised planter at the end. The lawn is now here to work for the garden, instead of the garden politely keeping guard at its edges.

When it comes to organic structure, it's easy to instantly think hedges! I removed the buxus hedging at the front of the house, a decision inspired by my desire to be a little more playful with my

When considering structure I find much of my focus is around juxtaposition...

hard
vs
soft

smooth
vs
textural

uniform
vs
organic

permanent plant features. Instead I planted an amalanchier tree and grasses, then took a gamble and have clipped sections of hedge into softly shaped masses – an experiment I am not yet sure is a success. Topiary balls have become a firm favourite of mine, with their smooth, curved surfaces adding an interesting contrast to the rigid edges of the brick elements and the softness of my seasonal planting. I have dotted them through the beds like comical full stops. They provide a moment for the eye to rest amid the sparse winter or chaotic summer. I've even let two bounce out of the garden to perch on the lawn, breaking up for a moment the smooth leading lines of the bed edges and green of the grass. The collection is mostly made up of excruciatingly slow-growing (and expensive), commonly used *Buxus sempervirens* balls, which I mixed with the faster growing (sometimes annoyingly so!) *Lonicera nitida*. They have all been moved around the garden multiple times and continue to thrive with no trouble.

And then there are the trees. I have removed many over the years, and the trees I have retained now have room to breathe and space to shine as important structure in my space. I find myself admiring the large old cherry and the intriguing twisted shadows it leaves across the lawn in the low winter sun. In spring it brings pom poms of popcorn blossom, in summer we gather gratefully in its shade, and in autumn its large broad leaves burst into flame. It is perhaps the most important and engaging element of organic structure on the whole property.

With more trees to purchase and plant, I am constantly on a hunt for specimens that offer both seasonal interest and also a natural maturing form that I feel will complement the vibe of what I am creating.

Next winter, take the opportunity to gauge the effectiveness of the structure in your own garden. Consider how you might improve the hardworking skeleton of your space, stocktake your mix of materials and look for spots where you can boost interest.

Opposite: My mother wandering under the wisteria-laden pergola at Winterhome garden. The clipped hedges and brick columns are the perfect foil to the soft, romantic blooms.

Watering in dry spells

PLANNING & PROTECTING YOUR GARDEN

Climatic conditions are tricky to foresee at the best of times, and with the projected volitility in our weather I have been thinking a lot about the make-up and position of my planting, considering ideas to safeguard it should we find ourselves experiencing very hot and dry summers.

In the years since I began my gardening adventure, I have come to realise that a good watering practice is all very well but tends to be a reaction to the season as opposed to getting ahead of challenging dry periods through good planting and preparation.

When I contemplate drought-resilient gardens (page 166), I immediately think of my friend Jenny Cooper of the inspiring Blue House in Amberley (page 246). Jenny takes water conservation seriously and has waded through years of research and experimentation to establish beds of beautiful but resilient plants that she resists watering wherever possible.

Over time I have banked a lot of valuable information from her staunch approach, and used it when designing my own beds.

Opposite: My niece Ada watering the cucumber by hand using tank-gathered rainwater from a barrel.

'If you can't give a plant water, give it shade'

JENNY COOPER

Two pieces of her advice – 'if you can't give a plant water, give it shade' and 'resist installing irrigation in new beds to avoid relying on it' – have bounced around my head with every decision I've made.

Recently I have been enlightened by the definition of two terms we gardeners tend to use interchangeably. When learning about plants that catch your eye or ones you are specifically investigating for climate-resilient beds, I've found it helpful to understand the important difference between those labelled 'drought tolerant' and those that are 'drought resistant'. The former refers to plants that have evolved to happily survive long periods without water, such as fleshy cacti and succulents. These are in slight contrast to drought-resistant plants, which will cope with extended periods of dry but, by nature, enjoy moderate watering, too, like many prairie plants.

Below is a list of plans and action that I have considered for my own garden in preparation for dry periods and water restrictions.

PLANNING FOR THE DRY

Do your research and observe the behaviour of your plants this summer: Ideally, you want to create beds with plants sharing the same watering needs. Even the best planning will reveal the odd sad and wilting specimen when the going gets tough, despite its neighbours holding strong. To avoid turning on the watering to appease a thirsty plant, instead look at places you might possibly be able to move it this autumn, where it will be in better company.

Start a good mulching practice now: Research your best-suited mulch and get onto this as soon as possible. For my small garden, I prefer pea straw as it is easy to handle and shift around my soft perennial planting. It also aids in enriching and loosening up my clay soil, helping with improved drainage over time, which many of my drought-resistant plants prefer. I mulch twice a year where possible, with a good layer (over 20cm) in spring and a top-up in late autumn as my perennials recede. Mulching provides an all-important barrier between your earth and the elements, vastly improving the condition of the soil and stopping it from drying out (page 80).

Considering shade: Rather than full shade, I refer to planted areas that might include airy trees in their midst that will take the sting out of intense midday or afternoon sun. If that's not an option, consider planting tightly or picking plants that create dome-shaped clumps to shade the earth below and reduce evaporation during the heat.

Water storage: There are many options available these days for capturing and storing rainwater that would otherwise disappear down the drain. At home, we have converted a wine barrel into water storage, utilising a basic downpipe diverter to fill up the tank when raining. While a single barrel wouldn't last all that long during water restrictions, it's certainly better than nothing and I have been surprised at how convenient it can be. With a simple dunk of my watering can, I can spot-water my cucumbers and tomatoes with little effort while avoiding turning on the irrigation system for my whole vege garden. It also feels very wholesome – and rainwater contains nitrate, which will make your plants glow with well-being!

Avoid pot city: As someone who gardened with an extensive collection of potted plants in my first few years, I can attest that they are very demanding in the height of a dry summer, often requiring daily or twice daily watering. This is due to most pots being made of porous materials which lose moisture through evaporation. If you thought a pet was a handbrake stopping you going on holiday, try gardening in pots! However, needs and wants may still call for pots so, where possible, try to utilise the biggest pots you can fit. I have also found that mulching around the potted plants has definitely reduced watering needs, making them slightly less of a pain.

WATER MANAGEMENT DURING THE SUMMER

Water deeply but less frequently: For ornamental beds, rather than having the irrigation set to come on daily at a certain time, physically monitor your garden by plunging a finger into the earth and considering its dampness. If it's dry at your fingertip, then watering will be called for.

Short, regular doses of water encourage plants to keep their roots near the surface, making them fragile, weak – and extremely reliant on you! Instead, once you have recognised the earth is dry, water your beds deeply for 45 minutes or so. Waiting for beds to properly dry out between watering encourages resilience in your plants and avoids overwatering, which can encourage disease.

At the height of a hot summer, during times of little to no decent rainfall, I try to water just once a week. Jenny Cooper, on the other hand, has some beds that can last 6–8 weeks and a few that never get watered at all. This is a lesson in plant choice, position and mulching techniques.

Know your plants: Vegetables are mostly much more thirsty than ornamental plants and they will demand more watering. When selecting drought-resistant plants, it's important to note that many of these may need a little more watering as they get established before reaching their resilient potential.

Water at the ends of the day: Watering in the morning before the intense heat of the day is best, however, evenings can be much more convenient for many. The main aim here is to avoid spraying your valuable resource into the midday sun, where it will evaporate at speed.

SECTION TWO

Tips &

tricks

Without a doubt, the most valuable knowledge I have accrued has been from other gardeners. The following pages offer tips and tricks that I have gleaned from my mentors, as well as those discovered through my own experiences of creating a garden as a beginner.

This section covers points that I wish I had been aware of instead of learning the hard way, and it's my hope they will help you avoid frustrating hurdles so you can continue with confidence.

TIPS & TRICKS

STILL

Stay a while, still.
Less like the wind,
more like the ground you stand on.
Where are you going anyway?
and what for? and must you?

The world that we live in moves
only as needed,
toward nourishment
toward light
toward life.
Save yourself for things that matter.

- Mary Walker

Starting a garden

THE BARRIERS & BREAKTHROUGHS

Recently, during a meandering chat with a friend, we strayed onto gardening, a topic new to our relationship of a decade or so. We talked about the lacklustre performance of some of her potted plants and I offered some advice based on my own trial and error.

We would never have had this conversation early in our friendship, a time when neither of us harboured much interest in growing beyond the odd indoor plant in our respective apartments. We wouldn't have made it past the confused, 'What do you think I should do?' stage either, as this was knowledge we didn't harbour. Yet, here we were now, with gardens and plant-based ideas that whirl around our heads at night and send us hunting for answers.

This conversation got me thinking about my own adventure from non-gardener to gardener. My path into a full-blown obsession for growing was entirely wound up in just two things: my stage in life, and property.

Up until the age of thirty-four, my adult years had seen me

renting and moving every three years. Not just house, but town and even island! My interest in spaces and design was fully focused on interiors, art and the precious possessions I could take with me. I did love being in other people's gardens, but domestic outdoor spaces were what I affectionally thought of as 'life background'.

In hindsight, my interests easily transferred to my current passion and pursuit of creating an ornamental, seasonal garden. But up until we purchased our Christchurch home, which had a garden (albeit spiky and evergreen), I had never had the urge to grow much of anything.

Now, what I previously considered 'life background' is one of my life's primary focuses! The garden is central to my creativity, well-being, connections and even work. From the comfortable, base level of experience I have now, it is easy for me to forget the blank-faced intimidation I felt at where and how to start. Back then, for the first time in my life, I had found myself ready to go with the space, the time and the existing inclination to research, but still felt that gardening was a foreign language that might just be too hard to learn.

Through doing, listening and reading I have built a bank of knowledge I couldn't have imagined would ever fit in my head! Perhaps the biggest lesson, however, is that I didn't need to know everything I do now to begin growing. And I will never be finished learning, as the constant discovery of gardening is what keeps me engaged. The understanding that I am only scratching the surface of the knowledge I can utilise both humbles and excites me.

After canvassing my garden friends and followers on Instagram about their perceived barriers to beginning to garden and the breakthrough discoveries that have kept them moving forward with their growing adventure, I realised how much in common we all had. Their responses, combined with my own experiences, have

helped me form what I hope is a reassuring list to give others the confidence to start their own garden.

BARRIER

Lack of knowledge.

DISCOVERY

Consider this: If gardening is so hard, then why is it that so many people do it?

The best way to learn is simply by doing. Through trial and error, you will rapidly gather relevant information as you grow. It's true, too, that with gardening comes new connections and resources that may not have been obvious before. You don't have to learn how to garden in isolation – ask family, friends and neighbours for advice. Staff at garden centres trip over themselves to assist new gardeners!

Type in the most basic of your questions online and be rewarded with free resources provided by gardeners the world over. YouTube, social media, websites and the library allow you to dip your toe into gardening as a beginner without investing too much time or money.

And remember that you have a partner in growing – Mother Nature. She takes care of most of it – you just need to learn the bare basics to get her started.

BARRIER

Lack of time.

DISCOVERY

Opposite: Clearing out my vegetable garden at the end of the season.

Gardening absolutely takes time. From preparing beds to starting seeds, transplanting and weeding, your garden also needs time to grow. While there is no instant gratification here, the enforced patience seems to have a magnetic appeal once you experience a successful result.

On reflection, the time spent in your garden is actually the point of it all. Ten minutes spent weeding or deadheading is ten minutes of self-care. Stolen moments of fresh air and your hands in the earth will change your life for the better. By all accounts, spending time working in the garden with children can also be a calming family activity.

Most importantly, your garden doesn't need you to tend to it daily! Plants want to grow and don't need supervision. If life leads you away for a while, you'll find that your garden is much more forgiving than you realise and getting it back on track isn't always the mammoth, painful job you imagine.

BARRIER
Expense.

DISCOVERY
Growing a garden can be as expensive as you want it to be. You have choices regarding the level of investment you want to make at every turn, with cost-saving options to take in nearly every aspect of growing. I find that money can sometimes save me time, but if I am patient, exactly the same results can be achieved by taking a cheaper, albeit slower, route.

If creating your first garden, start small. Garden in containers if renting or carve up a little piece of lawn to have your first go. Learning the difference between annual and perennial plants (page 20) can provide options for when you might choose to purchase or grow from seed. It can be vastly cheaper to grow from seed (page 62) but this takes more effort than plugging in purchased seedlings (page 258) or mature plants. Scanning the perennial table during autumn garden centre sales can reveal money and time-saving deals! (page 76). Many plants can also be harvested for cuttings, which you can propagate to increase your stock (page 70). And after a couple of years, many perennial plants can be dug up, divided and replanted to instantly bolster that plant's presence in your bed. The only expense here is time!

When buying tools, buy once by buying well (page 26). A good hand trowel will last you years – the cheapest one will bend at the first dig of a potato.

Below:
A combination of potted and planted dahlias makes for an abundant flower garden in a small area. **Next page:** Dahlias at dusk.

All in all, the biggest barrier I see in people choosing to start gardening, is they do not yet know the immense satisfaction and reward that awaits them. From their first homegrown salad greens to their first vase of flowers, surely gardening is the most beautiful and simple of life's pleasures.

Valuable advice for your first home
TIPS FOR MAKING INFORMED CHOICES

My gut feeling is that most first-home buyers are not experienced gardeners. From my own perspective, I can say that ploughing time and money into a rented outdoor space outweighed the benefits of getting into growing. Understandably, it's far more appealing to build a home with pieces that can be packed up and taken.

On arriving at a fresh property as an owner, where investment into the ground holds some new personal value, the potential can be overwhelming. Our first-time homeowner knows more than they care to admit about interest rates and very little about the seasonal behaviour of their inherited planting!

Here are some tips I have pulled together from my own experience of going from a renter to a home – and garden – owner.

ARM YOURSELF WITH BASIC BOTANICAL KNOWLEDGE

Before you spiral into feelings of intimidation or do something rash, take a moment to arm yourself with some basic information. To aid any future decision making you need an understanding of what is currently planted in your yard so that you can take sensible and cost-saving action. By grasping how perennial, annual, evergreen and deciduous plants work (page 20), you can take stock of what you have and decide what will stay or go. For example, many perennials can be dug up and moved, while any annual flowering plants you see will die away on their own.

TAKE STOCK

The urge to 'clear the section' on arrival is a common one, particularly for new homeowners with little growing experience. What you perceive to be a messy mass of planting might simply be a lovely garden that needs a light tidy-up! Remember, plants cost money and trees take years to mature, so before you impulsively dig, cut and chuck, you need to understand the benefits of what you are throwing out. Not to mention that if you remove a plant, something else will definitely pop up in its place – and it will be of the weedy variety.

Take the time to research and learn about what is already there before deciding what moves to make. By identifying the plants that thrive in your new space, you will be given clues as to what others you could add with success. Lure in a garden-minded friend (page 312) or neighbour with the promise of coffee and cake and get them to walk your borders, putting names to those foreign plants for you.

BE PATIENT AND DOCUMENT

One piece of garden advice I received was to wait a whole year before making any major changes to a newly purchased garden. Depending on the season you arrive in, the planting will not be fully revealed.

A deciduous tree in winter hasn't yet demonstrated its valuable shade in summer or appreciated autumn colour. Moving into a house in summer will give you a chance to see many summer flowering perennials, but you have no idea of the location of any spring bulbs that may be hiding below the soil. I speak from experience when I say you might arrive with a million ideas but don't yet have an understanding of the shady spots or lack of shelter that will affect your idealistic plans.

By all means, weed away, mulch your beds, cut back spent flowers and definitely take photographs to remind yourself of how the garden behaves in each season.

Best of all, by holding back you will get a firm grasp on how you actually use the existing space and gain ideas through this experience for future changes.

CONSIDERATIONS WHEN PLANTING

Once you feel you have a clear understanding of your microenvironment, you might start making some changes and additions. When choosing trees (page 196), research their mature size and be sure to plant with enough space in mind. Make sure you know where utilities are buried before you start digging and think about the planting distance from fences or gutters if that's relevant.

You might have moved into a new house where a developer has created some basic beds. Without fail, these tend to be too narrow to create nice layered garden planting, so perhaps you want to extend these before you start. Remember, gardens don't have to be laid out with straight lines!

While gardening might have previously held little interest, take your time to discover if this might be for you before googling 'low-maintenance planting'. There is no such thing as green space that doesn't need to be touched or monitored, so why not plant in a way that encourages you to engage with the roll of the seasons and offers you the pleasure of picking for your home, growing for your dinner and getting your hands in the earth every now and then.

What you perceive to be a messy mass of planting might simply be a lovely garden that needs a light tidy-up!

Mistakes I made as a new gardener
& WHAT I LEARNED FROM THEM

Even if you follow a recipe to the letter, your baking can emerge looking nothing like the picture. But with practice, you start to build knowledge and learn those little, passed-down tips and tricks that seem to make all the difference in arriving at a delicious success instead of a disappointing failure.

The same can be said for gardening. As a beginner, I have through experience slowly collected a list of mistakes to avoid making. Many gardening books never spell out what might be deemed 'gardening common sense', presuming you 'just know' if you are reading those pages. In an attempt to ease some pain for my fellow new growers, here are some harsh truths I have banked.

Previous page: Gathering up tree prunings in a large bag. **Opposite:** My now happy and healthy dwarf maple in the background with other potted trees and plants.

UNDER-WATERING AND OVER-WATERING

Both seem to be as brutal as the other and certainly are a blow to your motivation to learn about gardening at all. The best advice I ever had as a complete beginner was from a great garden centre staff member.

When I enquired about care for a certain plant she just said 'treat them like your babies'. Meaning, you can't just populate your garden and then walk away thinking the job is done. Regular check-ins will enable you to nurture your plant babies with life's basics, and this includes monitoring for dehydration and disease via saturation (page 96).

The easiest way to stay in the safe zone is to actively consider the week's weather, so you can water in reaction to it. If very wet, then don't continue your summer watering routine; give everything a breather to dry out a little. If extra hot and dry, then pop out and dip your finger into the soil to the first knuckle. If it feels moist at your fingertip, you are good for another day. If barely damp, it's time for a good soak.

It must be said that your watering should also respond to the type of plants you have. Learn the needs of what you are planting, and group them with others of similar watering requirements. This may lead to whole beds that don't need any additional watering at all (page 166).

IGNORING 'FULL SUN' LABELS

I will never escape the vivid memory of my first foray into flower growing, which resulted in my crop of larkspur growing horizontally to the ground. Desperately (and quite sadly, to be honest), they stretched out looking for sunlight from the shady bed I had planted them in.

As you progress and experiment, it's true you will find those sun-loving plants that don't mind some moments of shade during the day, but I now don't bother wasting my money or time trying to change the mind of Mother Nature. As a beginner, read the label and follow the directions.

NOT NIPPING SUPER-SPREADERS IN THE BUD

I cringe at the view of my cabbage tree being claimed by ivy; likewise the clover that has irretrievably entangled itself through my entire bed of violets. Yes, I saw these invaders in their early stages and no, I absolutely did not 'nip them in the bud' when it could have been a fast and easy job.

There is nothing fast and easy about righting these wrongs that I lazily watched happen. Wandering the garden and pulling these keen growers out at the roots in their youth would have avoided the headache I now have.

CUTTING CORNERS ON GARDEN BED PREP

I couldn't believe my luck when my bricklaying husband agreed to build me a raised, brick-lined bed in the sunny spot on the lawn. He beautifully constructed it, laid in irrigation, and even created a block support in the centre for me to position a potted tree. But I didn't pay attention to the soil that arrived home one day on the trailer ready for filling it. Soil is soil, after all? Wrong. I now spend each winter dressing it with quality compost and pea straw mulch to attempt to loosen up what is nasty, dense earth, difficult to dig in new plants and tough on seedlings forcing their way up to maturity.

NOT CONSIDERING PLANT HEIGHTS AND SPACING

In excitement, it's easy to poorly position those purchased, gifted or newly raised seedlings on your road to achieving your lush, full garden. However, not reading the labels or doing a quick search to reference mature size and height can really shatter that vision. Short plants behind tall, gappy or overcrowded beds (not in the artful way) are disappointing and can be so easily avoided.

It really helps to draw a basic plan detailing where you will position plants, noting their heights and recommended spacing so you don't get it wrong. When working with perennials, the first year might still look a little spaced out, but the second year will have you smiling into your camera lens.

NOT TAKING A CLOSER LOOK

We successfully transferred a dwarf maple from the garden into a wine barrel planter and I was almost disbelieving when it appeared to thrive. About four months later, in springtime, I noticed it was losing its newly unfurled leaves, looking shrivelled and generally sulky. From my beginner playbook, I simply couldn't work it out. I stepped up my watering, and applied plant food and still it was deteriorating.

Finally, I got really up close and personal, holding a branch at nose level, and slowly turning it over. This revealed an infestation of tiny mites sucking the lifeblood out of my little tree! I immediately searched online, found a remedy, and treated the tree – with the return to health being practically immediate.

The lesson here? Get out the magnifying glass.

Below: Placing irrigation into our new raised garden bed without realising our mistake of using soil that lacked good organic matter for vital drainage and health.

Soil is soil after all?.... Wrong.

A
VISIT
TO...

No. 11

The imagination-
capturing street
frontage of Robyn
Kilty's cottage in
Christchurch.

WITH
ROBYN
KILTY

A creative oasis

Before I was challenged with making my first garden, I was renting a tiny, modern home with my new boyfriend on the outskirts of the Christchurch CBD. Fresh off my move back to the South Island from Auckland, I loved to stalk my local streets, sucking in the dry Canterbury air and reacquainting myself with the old (or was it the new?) me.

My favourite streets, lined with tiny Victorian workers' cottages from the late 1800s, were just a few minutes' walk from mine, and I would drag my feet suspiciously slowly up and down the footpath taking them in. Amid all this architectural appreciation, there was one special property that sparked the tinder of my eventual gardening fire.

No. 11 demonstrated personality in every deliberate decision of its owner. There was the burnt orange front door, highlighted by the surrounding denim-coloured weatherboards. The wild, lawnless front garden towered over the jagged pail fence, deliciously

Opposite: The front door of the cottage with two *Pseudopanax crassifolius* (horoeka/lancewood) standing guard and an ornamental grape dripping from the veranda. The mosaic in the path was created by Robyn herself.

spilling plants up and over onto the narrow strip that pushed at the footpath. If I walked really slowly in springtime I could glimpse waterfalls of white wisteria beyond the back gate, while in autumn I'd admire the swathes of ornamental grape hanging from the front veranda, burning its way to brilliance.

At this point in time, I was struggling to keep herbs alive in pots, let alone to recognise and appreciate the progressive planting of this cottage's owner, but as my gardening interest ignited, so did my intrigue and determination to befriend this creative person who lived just around the corner!

If you have ever blamed a lack of space for limiting your gardening potential, I'm afraid to say Robyn Kilty is here to shatter your misconceptions.

In 1993 Robyn moved into the little cottage, then a sad, leaky version of itself. With much grit she inched it back to life, replacing the roof, remodelling the kitchen and bathroom, adding an art studio extension and peeling back layers of wall and paint to reveal honey-coloured kauri panelling. The interior speaks of her artistic eye as much as the garden does – rich in colour, art, books and collections.

The cottage didn't come with a lot of botanical flair, either. Long grass and two enormous, light-blocking pittosporums were the only plants growing in complement of a rickety aluminium shed around the back. In short, the scope was limitless!

Raised in a family of gardeners in Southland, Robyn's first distinct memory is of her grandfather holding her up to smell a rose. She has gone on to make gardens wherever she has lived and pre-earthquake, No. 11 housed a beautiful formal flower garden in an ode to the cottage's symmetry and history. The earthquake caused huge damage to her property, rendering it unliveable, sending Robyn to find some calm and refuge with her friend Penny Zino of Flaxmere garden in

North Canterbury (page 48), where she gratefully stayed for a year.

Fuelled by their mutual love of gardening and adventurous spirit, the pair made a trip to learn about naturalistic-style planting from Piet Oudolf in the Netherlands (page 174). It was a trip that ultimately turned a leaf in Robyn's personal gardening story.

She returned to No. 11 with fresh eyes and ideas, promptly banishing lawn and unnecessary paths from her garden. In a total transformation, the front bed was recreated with drifts of towering grasses and tall perennials in warm, rich tones. Texture, colour and form rise and fall from one season to the next, punctuated with the titivating structure offered by piles of topiary balls, intriguing towers of muehlenbeckia trained up stakes and beautiful mosaic work within the paths.

What fascinates me most, as a new gardener and former interior designer, is the masterful way Robyn has created zones in such a small space, working within a 314 square metre section, from which the cottage steals a generous footprint.

While the front garden draws any passerby to a standstill, through the back gate you are plunged into an extraordinary enclosed space. Burgundy iceberg roses and topiary play off against variegated flaxes and native ferns. It feels cool and secret, drawing you to the next 'room' beyond.

A pergola spanning the space between the house and fence offers you a grateful moment of shade. By summer, the great canopy of white wisteria has given way to a sheltering ceiling of foliage and dangling seedpods. A hand-formed mosaic fountain trickles water constantly, adding a natural soundtrack for the art studio opening onto it through French doors. In this space you could be anywhere in the world. And Robyn takes a more relaxed approach to maintenance: 'I like a certain amount of looseness and unruliness about my

If you have ever blamed a lack of space as limiting your gardening potential, I'm afraid to say Robyn Kilty is here to shatter your misconceptions.

Above: A brick pathway leads you past an inspiring mix of roses and native New Zealand plants.
Below: The compact back garden feels wild and abundant in spite of its small size.

garden, where I think many people are more interested in having a 'tidy' one. For instance – already wisteria leaves are turning gold and dropping all over my paving. I don't want to go out and rake them up, because to me they look natural and lovely lying on the brick-paved areas. When they turn brown and mushy – that will be the time to tidy them away.'

The back of the section is lined with two wide borders of mixed perennials and grasses cut through by a narrow paved path. Vegetables find their place amongst waving dahlias, fruit trees and rusty heads of orach. It feels romantic, modern and humming with life. 'I love the feeling of being engulfed by green and plants as well as naturalness! But to achieve this within a garden there is a certain amount of control required. As an artist I still need the colours and textures to blend together,' explains Robyn. 'Just because my garden space is small, I don't just want to use small plants. I want drifts of tall plants (perennials) amongst my small spaces and along the pathways, because I like to feel swamped and surrounded by plants and garden! Also, I like to plant my garden so that there is something of interest all year round. Gardening makes me feel happy and fulfilled and is also good exercise.'

Amid the millions of ideas that Robyn offers me in her vibrant urban garden is her reassurance that there is no one way to design a space or curate plants. That making a garden – of any size – should remain a personal and light-hearted journey. It is a creative endeavour that will continue to change course over the years.

'Making a garden is such a personal thing because we all visualise differently. For instance, many find great satisfaction in developing a smooth green sward of lawn, others from planting New Zealand natives, so that their garden reflects our native bush – all approaches are perfectly legit.'

Opposite: Vibrant dahlias glow against the blue exterior of the cottage.

Gardening tips from the wise

NUGGETS OF KNOWLEDGE

The only thing that is completely certain in gardening is that with time you will learn something. It is unavoidable, and this knowledge is quite reassuring for those of us starting out, wondering if it's possible to get a grip on any of it!

With that said, there are so many passionate gardeners in front of us that have already been banking knowledge, discovering helpful solutions and approaches that can make our own adventure a little easier from the start. I have had many a lightbulb moment when listening to general chat between long-time growers, so I thought I'd knock on the door of a few and find some tidbits to share here with you.

During one of the regular garden-based Q+As that I engage my mum in, she mentioned that a dash of neon spray paint on the handles of trowels and spades helps hugely in locating them during big garden cleanups. I instantly thought of the niwashi tool that I lost in my garden for a month, camouflaged in soil and leaves.

Jill Simpson of magical Fishermans Bay Garden on Banks Peninsula (page 180) offered me further guidance: 'When I was young and worked in a nursery, my boss said, "just learn one plant at a time", and over a lifetime that has added up. It's impossible to know everything, but accumulating that knowledge helps now as I look at what I want to achieve.

'My advice to new gardeners is to plant lots. As much as you can buy, beg or propagate, as only by growing something do you truly understand what it does and likes. You can always remove it, but plants take time to grow and there is never enough time.'

Deb Sisam of Puriri Lane Nursery in Drury had some great advice on planting to impart: 'One tip I got from my grandmother is when you are transplanting you should soak the plant in a bucket of water and wait until all of the bubbles disappear to ensure that the centre of the root ball is well watered before planting. I still do this today but have actually modified it a bit and use one capful of Seasol in a bucket of water, as

Opposite: A gardener's back door. Flaxmere garden, North Canterbury.

that really helps with transplant shock.'

Penny Zino of Flaxmere garden in North Canterbury commented further on planting, with the suggestion of, when possible, getting new plants in the ground in autumn instead of waiting until spring. This allows them time to settle and establish roots without the stress of dry periods that arrive with the warmer months. Penny also offered: 'Having a little place to pot up cuttings and new seedlings at bench height is also a game changer that can save a lot of money. I am loving my restored glass house with two benches at waist height, making it so easy to be there when the weather is cold. I am amazed at how many new plants I have created!'

Both Penny and Jennifer Horner from Puketarata Garden in Taranaki reiterate that mulching is something to get a handle on early. Compost is great for smaller urban gardens, while those mulching on a larger scale might find pea straw a more affordable option. Doreen and Mike Dryden from Loch Leven Garden in North Canterbury also demonstrated to me the great worth of linseed straw, which, being a little denser, doesn't get mucked around by birds to the same extent, or whisked away in a raging nor'wester!

It is ideal to get on top of mulching in autumn for the best preparation for springtime growth.

Michael Coulter, an experienced nurseryman and gardener who I met through the Canterbury Horticultural Society, offered terrific tips for gardening over winter. During frosty periods, avoid walking on lawn to avoid creating dark burn marks and in the wet, lay a plank of wood for walking on when harvesting veges to prevent the soil from getting compacted. Save pruning fruit trees and roses until conditions are dry to stop the spread of disease.

Lastly, some encouragement from fantastically creative gardener Robyn Kilty: 'It's about visualisation. Have a mental picture in your head of how you want the garden to look in the spring, and work towards that. This is especially applicable in winter when perennials have died down and the general green leafiness has gone, leaving the bones of your garden bare. It's at this time when you can really see your garden, warts and all, for what it really is. What you don't like and what you do! From here you can start to plan, imagine and visualise the difference and see in your mind how much better you can make it look for next season. And that's all about anticipation and imagination!'

In my experience, advice from gardeners that live in my own area is unrivalled in its relevance. But for those yet to make these connections, the internet and YouTube offer incredibly handy tips that might otherwise be left out of books.

It won't be long before you have helpful hints to share, too.

Below: Penny Zino wandering the paths at Flaxmere garden, North Canterbury.

Garden visits
Lessons Learned & Inspiration Gained

The further I got into my own garden, the more I noticed others. I became a keen observer of public planting and a very nosey neighbour as I walked my local streets. What people choose to grow in your area is an encouraging signal to you of what your environment and climate can offer your own space. What's more, you rapidly realise that the 'decorating' of a garden is not far removed from how people nest their own homes.

Plant choices and positioning can help you achieve the vibe you are after just as much as paint and furniture decisions inside. The weighty difference here is there are few opportunities for instant gratification; gardening revives your ability to display patience – an attribute that has disappeared over the years in this fast-paced era we live in.

It wasn't until I visited my first 'open' garden that I glimpsed the scale and potential of what a person can do with some earth. I was astonished at the realm I entered, and incredibly grateful to that family who chose to open to eager visitors. From here, I was hooked!

Opposite above & below: The fabulous grass and perennial border of Karen Rhind's garden outside of Cromwell.

Above: The dreamy spring wisteria show at Barewood garden in Marlborough.

As a beginner, I had been wrong in assuming garden visits and tours were only for experienced plant people. The discoveries I made, and continue to make as a newish gardener, have had an enormous bearing on my own creativity and bank of ideas. Since these first visits, I have become a serial attendee of garden tours and an eager explorer of open gardens, both on a small urban scale and sprawling rural scope.

I started trying to make sense of what I saw in these places created by everyday people with passion. What made lovely gardens into magical ones? What was preventing my own planting from appearing resolved and harmonious?

The realisation that gardens can impact my internal feelings in the same way great interiors and architecture do has been a big breakthrough in the way I consider outdoor spaces.

The following are some takeaways I have gathered from garden tours as a beginner on an adventure and journey of discovery.

REPETITION

I noticed that the gardens that I was most moved by had paid attention to repeating, grouping and re-weaving plants through beds to deliver on their aesthetic and style.

Lesson: Sometimes more of less is more.

STRUCTURE VERSUS SOFTNESS

For me, hard elements against soft planting is where 'design' enters my gardening equation, and it opens the doors to a lot of fun that even amateurs can experiment with. Consider bordering airy flower beds in brick or wood for contrast, or clipping shrubs into sculptural topiary.

Lesson: Juxtaposition is where the magic lives.

LINES OF SIGHT

Like great architecture, gardens can lead you through spaces and present special moments. I learned that this could be achieved in intimate gardens as much as sweeping ones.

Lesson: Atmosphere and drama can be achieved in any size garden once we consider how they might be viewed and moved through.

LAYERS AND TEXTURE

At the basic level, layers in a garden are likely created with planting shorter plants at the front and taller ones at the back. This is important for function and growth as much as the visual effect!

Richness and atmosphere can be created by layering textures across each other, considering a moment in the garden from the ground right to the horizon. This does require some experience in that you need to know what your mature plants will look like.

Lesson: Texture is just as important in a garden as it is in an interior.

Finding your community

CONNECTIONS TO AID YOUR GARDENING

As I moved through my formative gardening years, I began to notice the plentiful opportunities to gather locally with other gardeners. While I have found massive benefits in belonging to various garden-based groups on Facebook, it wasn't until I plucked up the nerve to attend my first meeting of the Canterbury Horticultural Society that I uncovered the real gold that I had been missing out on.

I took a seat at the back of the lovely kiosk in the Christchurch Botanic Gardens, well aware my red hair was intensely obvious among the more muted tones around me. The first presenter, Christine Blance of the Christchurch South Community Garden, gave a truly insightful talk about the garden's goals, sharing images of work parties, gatherings, community impact and the resulting fresh produce that was provided.

Next came Michael Coulter, delivering his informative monthly rundown of the recent weather conditions and excellent tips on what could be done around a garden at that specific time of year.

There were no complicated, isolating words. No questions were too simple. The experience wasn't what I had expected at all!

It was immediately clear to me that the CHS was as relevant to me as a new gardener as it was to the members who'd had their hands in the earth their whole life. But where were my fellow beginners?

Limited time is always the first factor in passing membership options by, and at various stages of their lives people are busy with work commitments, children's commitments, young families and otherwise full lives. Time – and perhaps the fact that we can so readily source information in the sporadic moments available to us via our phones, the internet and the sofa at the end of a long day.

Is it that we feel we have less time than the generations above us did at the same age? Or is it just that, within our peer groups, there

Opposite: The iconic dahlia beds at the Christchurch Botanic Gardens, where the Canterbury Horticultural Society is based.

isn't that lead to follow into clubs? When considering those I know in their thirties and forties, I would hazard a guess that if any did belong to a club, outside of their friendship groups, it would likely be related to sports, snow, wine or craft.

On one occasion I was invited to share my story of transforming from a non-gardener to an obsessed one at a meeting of the Friends of the Gardens, a volunteer group created to foster the important link between the Christchurch Botanic Gardens and the community, whilst also supporting the gardens team in maintaining this great public asset.

Once again, mingling with fellow gardeners, I was not only reminded of the powerful positivity a shared passion has in fostering connection but also the glaring fact that age should be no barrier. It is true that retirees have the opportunity to commit more time toward gathering or volunteering, hence why so many of these groups are attended by people senior to us. In this respect they also have more capacity to lend you their experience and advice and, to me, that's the absolute advantage of it all! These multi-generational groups offer us newbie gardeners access to knowledge, support and enthusiasm that would be missing if we were surrounded by only our peers.

I, too, juggle my work and home responsibilities but have picked gardening as a passion I am willing to squeeze in. While I only slip into a CHS meeting every so often, I always leave feeling rewarded, inspired, and amped on improving my attendance.

In my experience, the gardeners above me provide all the answers to the sticky little questions I have about my own home plot. And I can only encourage other new gardeners to dip their feet in and slide into their local meeting too.

As someone who is very protective of her free time, I'd like to dismantle this fear of commitment that can act as a deterrent to club membership. Garden clubs, societies and groups of all shapes and forms present us with opportunities that we can simply match to the commitment we are capable of and the area of our interests.

For instance, the Canterbury Horticultural Society holds two meetings a month. One in the evening and, in an effort to be flexible, the other mid-morning the following day. These meetings always involve invited speakers followed by garden advice and are just one part of a very active, wider offering of workshops and activities arranged by the society. All of these can also be attended by non-members, with a small fee.

Becoming a volunteer at a community garden will require occasional donated time and muscle, but in return, you will receive free mentorship and guidance, which you gain while building on your garden skills. No experience is required and the connections and learning are limited only by your availability.

Garden clubs are focused on arranging speakers, demonstrations or garden visits for their members while offering comradery and casual connections. These positives are invaluable to beginners that might not have people within their family or friendship groups who are also interested in growing.

Wondering how you might discover gardening clubs or societies nearby? A quick online search will bring up information about neighbourhood and regional garden clubs and community gardens in your area, right across the country. It's probably not the sort of thing you will see promoted posts advertising on our Instagram feed and unless a friend pulls you in, it can be easy to miss their presence. But it would be such a shame to overlook their benefits to our own gardening adventure where local knowledge can be so easily garnered and some new friendships might spring from it.

Photographing your garden

TIPS TO CAPTURE THE MAGIC

A really satisfying part of my gardening adventure has been documenting the progress as I go. Looking back at photos of my first-year planting, I can remember my thrill at the humble petunias and cosmos blooming. I feel continually amazed at the journey my garden has gone through from then to now, and my backlog of images is a lovely reminder of just how far this obsession has taken me!

My love of photography is very much buoyed by having a garden and, as my skills at growing have increased, so has my passion for getting creative with the camera. Free of any expectations that a professional photographer might be compelled to meet, the quiet time spent snapping my flowers and garden beds has become a creative hobby in which I revel in experimentation.

This regular documentation has also aided my gardening knowledge and connection to the life cycles happening in my own backyard. Not only has every year seen a vast transformation in my

Opposite:
Getting up close and personal in the flower beds, finding focus beyond the closest plants.

garden as a whole, but each passing season has also offered visual treats to be collected and remembered, too.

When planning for the future, I can easily refer back to my library of images to gain a better understanding of how much light an area receives, which is vital for my planting combinations. I can also compare the size of trees to gain knowledge on their rate of growth, and the noticeable improvement in plants that I have moved to better positions. It is very satisfying to have these visual references at hand.

Above: Allowing surrounding foliage to creep into images can help pull the viewer right into the space. **Next page:** Backlighting plants in soft natural light can make for magical images.

My urge has always been to capture atmosphere and a sense of place beyond a simple, straight-up snapshot. There is so much fun to be had with this! Over the years I have collected and developed my own set of basic skills to help me photograph my garden's magic in reflection of how it feels at the time. It's my hope the following tips will aid you in your own practice, whether you prefer to reach for your camera, phone or tablet

FIND THE LIGHT

The softness and lower angle of the sun in the morning and late afternoon provides the garden with a glow that invites me to use this light to my advantage. I like to point my lens towards it, using it to backlight specific plants or beds. I enjoy moving my camera around to allow shafts or dots of light into the frame, without completely washing out the photo. I love nothing more than a plant specimen traced in golden lines by the sun pushing through from behind.

FIND YOUR FOCUS

Before you snap your image, first be sure that your device is focused on the area you want to highlight. On a camera using autofocus, this will often be found by training and adjusting a green square to lock onto your subject with a half-press of the button. On a phone or tablet, you can tap the subject on your screen to pull it into focus. If taking a wider shot of a garden bed, tap or select a spot in its midst and take a few shots to be sure you'll have one that works.

Get up close and personal with your plants, find your focus and be amazed at the delicious results when your device automatically reduces the depth of field. I encourage those using a phone for photography to explore the portrait mode option for this, too.

CHANGE YOUR POINT OF VIEW

Extend yourself from photographing only at standing height and get exploring your garden from all angles. I find myself balancing on the edges of my raised beds to shoot from above, dropping a knee to look 'through and up' plants, and wading into beds to find a different aspect from within their midst. I even prefer it when out-of-focus greenery cuts through a shot – it pulls me further into the final image.

I love nothing more than a plant specimen traced in golden lines by the sun pushing through from behind.

USE YOUR LEGS TO ZOOM

If you are using a phone or tablet, I would suggest you resist using your fingers to zoom and instead take progressive photos as you physically move closer to your subject. Even though technology has improved in leaps and bounds, unless you are using a late-model device, a 'zoomed in' image is never as crisp. If you're using an actual camera this doesn't apply – zoom away!

LOOK FOR YOUR LINES

One of the easiest ways to improve your photo-taking is by allowing time to ensure any hard line is level. This might be a fence, the horizon, or a raised planter running through the background of your frame. Don't forget your vertical lines, too, like doorways or veranda posts – I angle my camera and body forward/back, up/down until the line runs nicely parallel to the screen. If I find that I haven't got it right when reviewing my images later, I use my phone's inbuilt editing software (or an editing app) to adjust the tilt and resave it.

Opposite: Sometimes you need to step right into the garden to capture dreamy moments. **Next page left:** Play around with the height from which you take your photographs. Here I crouch in a grass-lined pathway to deliver a sense of place. **Next page right:** Pay special attention to getting horizontal and vertical lines straight and square in your image.

CONSIDER YOUR COMPOSITION

If we never stopped to think about our shot, it would only be natural to place a subject in the middle of the frame. However, playing around with moving it off-centre can often make for a more visually appealing result.

When composing your shot, mentally break your screen into thirds, both horizontally and vertically. Aim to place your subject along the lines or at the intersection of each third instead of smack in the centre. It is very helpful to turn on the 'grid' option on your phone and camera to assist in getting used to composing using these zones. It will then become innate!

SECTION THREE

Plantir

In this section you will find introductions to planting styles and considerations you can make based on your environment.

I profile some of my favourite plant types as well as bloom shapes that can add delicious interest to your beds. There is a strong focus on planting for a drifting seasonal show, allowing you to appreciate the beauty of your plants in all stages of their life cycle.

PLANTING

WALK GENTLY

Slow down.
Press lightly with your feet.
Shoes on, shoes off, it doesn't matter.
The land just wants to hold you.

Feel the air
brush your cheeks as you go,
welcoming your breath,
folding it back into itself

even as it rushes to fill you again,
settling in the cup of your ear,
in the space between lashes,
running, like a hand, over your hair.

- Mary Walker

Climate-resilient gardening
PLANTING IN RESPONSE TO YOUR ENVIRONMENT

Revered British gardener Beth Chatto (1923–2018) was a pioneering voice in the concept of 'right plant, right place', an approach that urges gardeners to avoid forcing plants into an environment, climate and position they don't like, instead taking stock of the site and actively selecting specimens that will thrive there. She demonstrated this by transforming a carpark and a section of scrubby wasteland on her property from gravelly, dry soil combined with waterlogged areas into thriving gardens, full of plants naturally adapted to cope with these conditions. Her book *The Dry Garden* is still readily reached for by gardeners across the world.

Here in New Zealand, I have explored many diverse dry gardens, inhaling their aesthetic and finding myself intrigued by each gardener's planting and approach. These are gardens that have a spare elegance, a beauty that feels slow and calm.

I remember visiting two extraordinary gardens in Cromwell, a place renowned for its stony ground, painfully hot and dry summers and equally painfully freezing winters. With lots of watering and maximum composting, it would be possible to plant a traditional ornamental garden here, but as I found out, there are equally attractive alternatives to be considered.

Top horticulturist Jo Wakelin chose to create a garden for herself, never with the intention of opening to the public, but as a personal pathway through some tougher times. The resulting work has received international acclaim for its sustainable approach and seasonal display.

It is a garden that receives zero watering support; instead Jo has applied a thick layer of gravel as protective mulch. Much of her garden is made of hardy plants that hump and mound around each other in reflection of the dramatic borrowed landscape.

Opposite: Vibrant but resilient plant choices made by Jenny Cooper at the Blue House in Amberley, North Canterbury.

'My landscape was created to fit as subtly as possible into the awe-inspiring surrounds and a harsh, dry climate,' shares Jo. 'I wanted to incorporate strong design with plants that could thrive without any watering where the annual rainfall can be as low as 280mm. For me, it is also an expression of a range of emotions. I feel the shakkei principle [the ancient technique of incorporating the landscape into a garden] tied the garden to its surroundings which I find so beautiful.'

In contrast is Karen Rhind's garden down the road. Here I fell in love with her tall border of grasses mixed with tough perennials, which receive a little additional watering on top of low natural rainfall – though her use is still far below traditional watering practices.

Neither garden looks or feels familiar in comparison to most New Zealand gardens but they both reflect a style and attitude of planting that has gained great traction in other parts of the world, particularly those that share similar climates to New Zealand, such as parts of Spain.

Gardener Jenny Cooper of the Blue House (page 246) learned the lessons of considering her site the hard way. Moving to dry and windy Amberley in North Canterbury, she created her garden from scratch, using common practices learned over many years. But over five years, despair set in as she watched her heavily composted beds whip up and away in the howling nor'wester. Stressed plants withered in the dry heat and she grew tired of racing around with a hose as much as staking waterlogged plants when rain did arrive.

After much research, she formed a new strategy for planting resilient beds suited to her area and is well on her way to her goal of having half of her large garden exist water-free, with no rain, for six weeks to three months in summer. What's more, these dry beds are tough – they remain undamaged by screaming winds, and have no fungal disease.

I asked Jenny to share some of the techniques she considers most important for those looking to start a resilient garden. She obliged with enthusiasm.

DON'T DIG

When creating new beds in lawn or ungardened ground, cover the area with cardboard to kill the grass and mulch heavily to a depth of 24cm or more to completely block out the light. Leave fallow for a few months if possible. When it comes time to plant, move the mulch back, plant at soil height and replace the mulch around your tiny specimen. Jenny also readily plants directly into the lawn soil with no turning over or cultivating.

PLANT SMALL

Skip the $150 trees and buy the $30 whips! By using young plants, you harness their youthful vigour. Their early growth spurt needs to happen in your soil rather than the pot so that they form the best root system they are capable of. Ideally, when planting in autumn and winter, plant with bare roots. Shake off potting mix (which dries and wets at different rates to native soil), cut off girdling roots (those that grow in a spiral or circular pattern, and can gradually strangle the trunk), and spread the rest. Small plants cope best with bare rooting, as they are still in a vigorous growth stage and will adapt to their new ground with greater ease than large plants that will struggle to establish while supporting their existing limbs and leaves.

GROW THE SOIL

Jenny's focus is on mulch, adding no other soil amendments, even when planting. Young plants will initially live on the dead roots of grass, which also contribute to excellent, humus-rich soil.

Next page: The fascinating dry mounding beds in autumn at Jo Wakelin's Central Otago garden.

Intact, healthy soil contains mycorrhizal fungi that form symbiotic relationships with most plants, bringing them water and nutrients in exchange for carbon. Once a plant has mycorrhizal input, it is much more resilient to drought.

'I wanted to incorporate strong design with plants that could thrive without any watering where the annual rainfall can be as low as 280mm'

JO WAKELIN

AVOID BARE SOIL AT ALL COSTS

As Jenny points out, in nature, bare soil never really occurs, with weeds quickly moving in. Her preferred mulch is ramial woodchip (made from mulched up branches, leaves and all), which encourages the mycorrhizal fungi. She also uses river stones, pine needles, grass clippings – anything to cover the soil. These mulches keep the moisture in and stop the weeds. Weeding is not an issue in her garden.

PLANT IN ZONES

The biggest lesson Jenny learned was to strictly plant in zones. Each year she is on the lookout for plants in the wrong place, either shifting them or giving them away. Putting the hose on dry-loving plants such as salvias, lavender and sedum makes them soft and disease-prone, so it is not ideal to have one thirsty plant in their midst.

Below: Jo's resilient planting in spring.

The New Perennial Movement

A BASIC INTRODUCTION

I can remember arriving at the 'design' phase of my gardening life.

After stumbling into the 'have a go' chapter, I graduated to the 'education' stage, which segued into the 'collector' period, resulting in a garden that resembled a living library of all my favourite plants in a somewhat chaotic but lovable mish-mash. Then, I turned toward the hunt for atmosphere.

My passion for growing has led me to visit many fantastic New Zealand gardens, vastly different from each other but with a feeling of cohesiveness and intention that I began to recognise was missing from my own patch. I've come to appreciate that experienced gardeners reflect their personal style with plant curation to achieve atmospheres that might be considered traditional, structured, wild or whimsical – an approach that is also achieved with architecture and interior decoration. Varying use of hard landscaping, trees, shrubs, seasonal flowering plants and layout builds on this style, providing endless opportunities to present the viewer with a sense of occasion, whether it be formal, casual or somewhere in between.

Inspired by some specific gardens and the fabulous central-city planting in Christchurch, I found a particular design movement that really attracted me. The New Perennial Movement, with its naturalistic planting style, has a foot in ecology, site-specific planting and celebrating plants as features throughout each stage of their lifeline. Overall, it is an effort to create gardens that both mimic and are in unity with nature. Interpretations of this concept are wide and varied, allowing ideas to evolve as factors such as climate change and the needs of local ecosystems are drawn into question.

Northern Hemisphere examples (where the style has had a long foothold in Europe, the UK and North America) commonly weave soft grasses through drifts of flowering perennials, chosen to deliver interest as the seasons progress.

Points of focus are provided by introducing a variety of form and colour through blooms, seedheads and foliage resulting in a kind of large-scale, artful, living tapestry. There is an emphasis on appreciating a changing garden-scape throughout the year, with no rush to chop and tidy in autumn; instead, a New Perennial or 'naturalistic' garden encourages the onlooker to find beauty in the skeletal, textural and muted scene the planting finds in the seasonal cooling. A thorough cutback then usually occurs in late winter.

Beyond the initial visual results, principles of value for those designing these gardens are in mixing together plants that respond well to their specific environment and ground conditions, planting tightly to reduce opportunities for weeds, and providing a living habitat to support insects, pollinators and birds.

While everything is planted with intention, the aim is to offer an impression that this space has occurred 'naturally' – which is almost never the case, given that the plants used are often interesting exotics

Next page: The wild and beautiful naturalistic-style planting at Flaxmere garden, using hardy plants that still provide a seasonal show.

mixed with natives of the region.

As garden designer and writer Robyn Kilty shared with me: 'Naturalistic gardens are those that look as though they have just appeared in a natural landscape. However, a garden, whether it is called naturalistic or not, by the mere fact of being a garden is always moulded by humankind and not nature. It is actually a style designed by people to look natural, even though it has not evolved naturally.'

Intrigued by this fresh style of planting, six years ago Robyn, along with fellow celebrated gardener Penny Zino, set off for The Netherlands and a workshop with the designer best known for spotlighting and expanding the concept in recent times, Piet Oudolf. His name is the first that springs to mind for many when discussing the New Perennial Movement, and he is the creator of world-famous examples that include The High Line in New York, Hauser and Wirth in England and his own garden of forty-plus years at Hummelo in The Netherlands.

The pair sought to understand the principles of the approach, which differed greatly from the traditional European styles that arrived in New Zealand with colonialism, and how these might be translated into their South Island spaces. Robyn has a very compact urban garden in Christchurch, and Penny a 3.2 hectare rural garden in North Canterbury. Penny says: 'I love the softness and the etherealness of naturalistic gardens. The naturalistic approach seemed so much more flexible and suitable to our conditions. In my case, nothing over a metre was the general rule, otherwise it would be flattened in the winds we have.

'It is a way of gardening that can be so individual and therefore can be suited to a range of conditions. I love the way it moves in the wind, the grasses coming into their flowering season add so much, and later with seedheads forming, it is magical.

'All this can be done using our native grasses, which is another reason it appeals as these gardens will take on a different look to what you see in Europe or other places. It can feel as if it belongs here. I love the individuality of the different colours of the perennials winding their way across an area.'

She has encountered challenges along the way as she tweaks and experiments with her naturalistic beds. There's been problematic self-seeding of some plants, versus the shorter lifespan of others, and the need to combine plants that have the same water requirements in the interests of using as little water as possible, which is also a top priority of the concept. Even, on reflection, realising that her initial planting wasn't tight enough to work against weeds. As she admitted, this is all part of the spontaneous nature of the approach and the constant balancing act of exploring gardening.

While some of the Northern Hemisphere interpretations are a closer reflection of naturally occurring wild areas of those regions, Robyn rightfully points out that a New Zealand example of a naturalistic garden 'would more likely be a garden of native trees and shrubs as we see in our native bush, where most species are unique and endemic to New Zealand and nowhere else.'

We have very few native flowering perennials and most of those that do flower tend toward white, so this presents a challenge in creating the attractive blend that is a hallmark of this style. Therefore, mixing our natives with exotic plants reveals great creative potential.

Exploring the principles of the New Perennial Movement allows me to fully embrace the idea that I can use my garden to reflect my personal style and vision. As always, it will be a matter of keeping up the research of plants, accepting the volatile and experimental nature of working with living things, and remembering that the process is as creative and rewarding as the eventual results.

Something we should all relish.

A VISIT TO...

Fisherm[an]s Bay

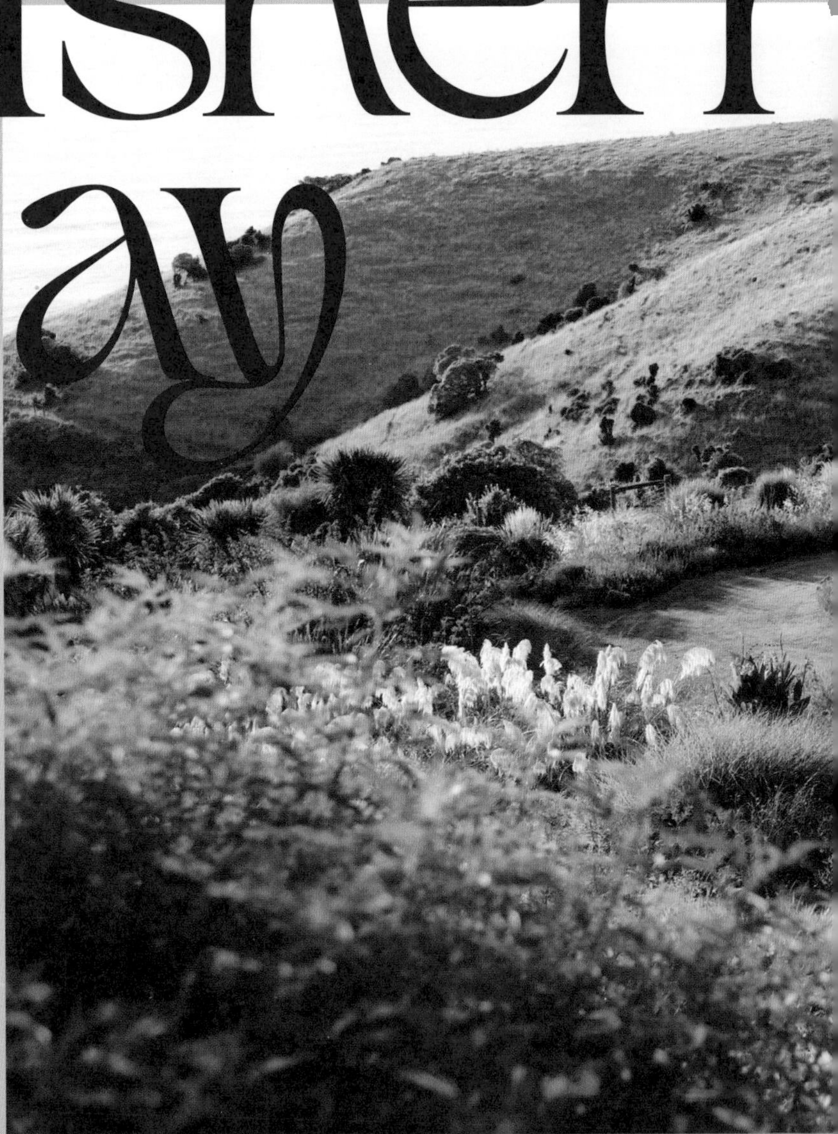

Fishermans Bay garden sits high on the eastern edge of Banks Peninsula, Canterbury.

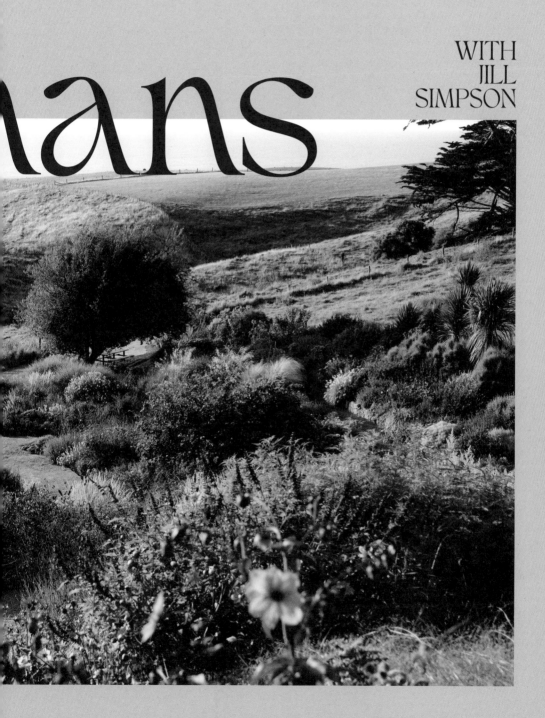

WITH JILL
SIMPSON

ans

A coastal kingdom

As readers of an Italian magazine poured over beautiful images of Banks Peninsula garden Fishermans Bay in early 2022, they were in blissful ignorance of the atrocious summer Jill and Richard Simpson had been experiencing.

The narrow winding road that regularly led buses of domestic and international garden tourists down from the peninsula's spine to Fishermans Bay was all but destroyed in late 2021, during the biggest storm event in decades. Finding themselves cut off as they scrambled to get home from a visit to nearby Akaroa, the pair abandoned their vehicle and negotiated the steep climb down in torrential rain. They spent hours precariously skirting slips that had carried their only road in away down the gully. With their home completely cut off for a week and the access gate padlocked as a closed road for many more, the Simpsons were grateful for their generator and helicopter drops of provisions, knowing neighbouring bays were worse off than theirs.

The Simpsons shared this story as I sat guzzling elderflower cordial after a morning spent photographing the breathtaking magic of their garden at dawn. It was hard to imagine the large tumbling beds of naturalistic planting clinging on for dear life as a torrent of water attempted to wash it all down to the sea. Instead, I had sat in the stillness of twilight, listening to bulls roaring at each other across paddocks and the magpie chorus counting me down for the sun's breach of the horizon. The orange beams finding their focus and touch on the South Island, choosing to be here first each day before any other point.

As it is today, the garden is settled across approximately two hectares of steep, east-facing hillside. While it is mostly frost-free, drought and wind provide the most regular challenges. These are followed by occasional bouts of catastrophic wet, as was demonstrated that summer.

Giant macrocarpas shield the garden's back, supported by the undulations of the land, pockets of mature native bush, and a

Opposite: New Zealand native *Cordyline australis* (cabbage tree/tī kōuka) dot their way through the garden to the steep shores of Banks Peninsula.

crisscrossing grid of terracing and paths. Unable to be viewed in full
from any single point, this is a rewarding garden to explore, moving
from the wide traditional perennial border to the outstanding swathes
of hebe planting, cool native forest, and cascading naturalistic beds
that rest across the hill like a tapestry.

Jill Simpson has attached herself to gardens and the natural world
her whole life. As a country girl surrounded by nature, she spent more
time on the moss garden around her dolls' house than the house itself.
As she matured, her passion for gardening was only tempered by her
passion for art. She studied fine art and art history between children,
moving on to landscape design and landscape architecture papers
that allowed her to work as a designer while raising her family as a
single mother.

On meeting Richard Simpson twenty-five years ago, the couple
would split their time between their Christchurch-based families
and their peninsula property, driving backward and forward until
their children had grown and Fishermans Bay could become their
full-time base. In those busy years, the garden was comparably low-
key to match their schedule. Over time, they extended the garden
out from the house, with the planting and tone a reflection of Jill's
interests at each stage.

Passionate about their area's natural heritage, they planted pockets
of natives, initially picking only from the palette of plants that chose
to grow there naturally. Extending from this, they planted further,
using natives from all corners of the country.

Inspired by the meadow and prairie plantings of the Northern
Hemisphere, Jill sought to reinterpret this style through the substantial
use of hebes. She admits that her vision was never truly achieved
by using the native flowering shrubs for this concept, frustratingly
curtailed by gaps when a plant failed for any given reason.

'Each new area reflects a time in my gardening evolution. The soil and shelter available provided challenges and opportunities, dictating what could be grown and what I could manage to maintain. All new gardens present a gardener with much more of a challenge while they establish. One of the joys of gardening is that one is always learning,' shares Jill.

Below: Exotic planting meets New Zealand natives.
Next page: Jill Simpson's sprawling naturalistic area spreads like a tapestry across the hillside.

As her experience and understanding of her environment grew, Jill turned her hand toward mixing natives with exotic plants. This was a chance to reignite her long-held passion for perennials and the establishment of a new area of garden inspired by the planting philosophies of the New Perennial Movement (page 174).

This part of the garden seems to sing with the seasons, moving through fresh spring greenness, saturated patchworks of summer

colour, and the long-limbed, rich tones of autumn. Come winter it is a sea of shifting texture, neutral and fascinating in its quiet state before being cut back, ready for the cycle to begin again.

As Jill explains: 'This garden gives me a wonderfully complex and challenging way to express the creativity that I think lies within my personality. I love the planning and the searching for new and interesting plants and ideas. I love the making and the weeding and am at my happiest working outside in the garden. Then there is the deep satisfaction and joy I feel when all of the things that make gardens happen come together. Like nature, the weather, a burst of inspiration or chance in the form of a seedling aligning successfully to be experienced by me, by Richard, and by the visitors to the garden.'

Fishermans Bay is an extraordinary garden in an extraordinary place.

Below: Native and exotic planting create secret shady areas to explore as you criss-cross the hillside garden.

'This garden gives me a wonderfully complex and challenging way to express the creativity that I think lies within my personality'

JILL SIMPSON

Cut and come again
PLANTS THAT JUST KEEP GIVING

I am still surprised by what nature gets up to in my humble backyard plot. But no surprise has been better than the discovery of plants that fall into the category of 'cut and come again'. They are the extra value, bonus-giving rewards to anyone wanting a flower-filled garden.

In short, 'cut and come again' refers to plants that will continue to flower if you prevent them from forming seedheads, at least until the first frost or disease claims them. By consistently harvesting their flowers for the vase or 'deadheading' their dying ones, the denying of any chance to create seed triggers them to have another go at producing new flowers. An excellent and rewarding result for you, the gardener!

The process of deadheading refers to snipping off faded, wilting blooms. Cutting flowers for the vase has the same effect, you are just removing fresher ones from the plant. Deadheading is made easy with an early evening stroll, armed with narrow-nosed snips and a bucket for your victims, or simply let them fall to the earth after cutting, where they will decompose and help your soil along.

For most 'cut and come again' plants, look to snip the flowering stalk off as close to the main stem as possible, or, if it is the whole central head of the plant, snip off between a pair of leaves or just above a side stem. It's in these intersections that new growth springs if it hasn't already!

Some of my favourite annual plants that you would manage in this way are cosmos, snapdragons and zinnias. Perennials like dahlias, penstemons and salvia are the gifts that keep giving into autumn.

Sweet peas are perhaps the best surprise here, responding magnificently to diligent harvesting and deadheading (page 192). The great Monty Don once noted that if you head out and harvest every single open bloom on your vines one to two times a week, leaving only unopened buds, your gorgeous sweet peas will continue to flourish far beyond the limited natural cycle that occurs once seedheads have developed. This is a theory I have tested with great success.

Among the 'cut and come again' family, roses have perhaps posed the biggest challenge for me as a beginner as they have a slightly different set of rules when encouraging their ongoing show.

For floribunda types that have an abundance of blooms on a single stem, you can visit them weekly to simply snip off the wilted, petalless heads, leaving their healthy neighbours and buds intact. Once a whole head of blooms looks done, snip off the flowering stem just above the closest five-fingered leaf. This sounds weird, but is obvious once you start counting those leaf fingers! Aim to make a clean cut on a 45-degree angle just above the leaf, as this helps with water running off and avoiding disease. You will notice a tiny little red bud already forming in that intersection; this will become your new flowering stem. Like magic!

If your bush starts looking a little wonky in shape, it is okay to take your deadheading down to the second five-fingered leaf – I have found my roses respond just as well to that. My iceberg roses will flower right into winter if I keep on top of deadheading.

In short,
'cut & come again'
refers to plants
that will continue
to flower if you
prevent them
from forming
seedheads,
at least until
the first frosts.

For hybrid tea roses that usually have one bloom per stem, you want to only snip off just above the first five-fingered leaf to encourage another go. It is incredibly satisfying to see the fresh new growth firing away for round two! To add a twist to this, many heritage species roses will only bloom once in spring, so deadheading is not required and allowing the seedheads to form will reward you with magnificent hips in autumn.

So if you are looking around your new patch of flowers, wondering how each of your plants will respond, I would suggest a quick google to see if they are referred to as 'cut and come again'. Knowing what you can harvest harder for your inside posies is very helpful, and keeping flowers around for as long as possible in your garden makes all the effort worth it.

Below left: Deadheading some types of roses pushes them to produce new flowers. **Below right:** Fresh growth on a deadheaded floribunda rose.

Trees and your garden

MANAGEMENT, PLANNING & PLANTING

Moving to a new property and garden can be as exciting as it is overwhelming. With only a little gardening experience under your belt, it's easy to walk your inherited borders with an eye for a clean-up. Gnarly old trees might look messy and pointless, particularly when viewed in winter, and the urge to clear the section can be hard to resist.

Over the years I've slowly pulled trees from the background of my interest to the front. My learning and understanding of how they play into a garden environment has increased, mostly due to the deep questioning I force on those with experience! I have learned – from my own tree clearing – the pros and cons of losing privacy to gain sunlight and have found a new love of multi-stemmed trees like amelanchiers and even my limbed-up camellia.

A few years ago, I invited Chris Walsh, managing director of Treetech, to join a panel I was running so that he could share his wealth of knowledge with my interested audience. I will never forget his first and most important piece of advice.

Opposite: The felling of a diseased old plum tree in my garden.

He urged new homeowners to wait a year after moving into a property before cutting down any trees. This allows sufficient time to see what the trees offer to the section throughout the seasons and gives a full understanding of each one's value to privacy, shade and aesthetics. Given the many years a tree might take to grow to useful maturity, the knee-jerk reaction of removing it without any understanding of its advantages can lead to regret only cured by expense and patience.

Below Chris shares some fantastic advice that can save us all from making rash, expensive mistakes.

BEFORE REMOVAL, DO YOUR RESEARCH AND OBSERVE

Find out the names of each tree on your property. Discover its seasonal behaviour, environmental needs and eventual mature height. The ugly tree in the corner that doesn't appeal to you might also be blocking a direct view from your neighbour's window. Its looming size in winter might make it feel cold, yet in summer it provides welcome shade for your home or garden. Maybe it is yet to reveal a stunning display of spring blossom or autumn colour that you haven't witnessed. Or the tree's form might be sheltering you from strong prevailing winds and its removal might expose you or create a wind tunnel through those left behind. All in all, a little patience and study will help you avoid mistakes.

BEFORE BREAKING GROUND

Before taking spade to ground and popping a friendly-looking young tree in your garden, there are a number of factors to consider.

Research your chosen tree's eventual height and span, avoiding the risk of introducing a monster into a petite space! It's equally important to consider its canopy and how this might encroach on your neighbours' property or push at your boundary fence. Is it evergreen or deciduous? Will it drop fruit and leaves over the fence or into your gutters?

Importantly, save yourself further costly mistakes by knowing exactly where services like power, fibre, phone or water pipes are positioned.

CHOOSING A TREE

To begin with, research options that answer your needs around space, preferred aesthetic and shade. Personally, I have found valuable benefit in questioning specialist garden centre staff on this.

When selecting a tree from a nursery, look for one with a good strong stem and a nice central leader. You want a tree that isn't root bound and is clearly labelled. While it's tempting to pick up discounted trees, usually this means they are old stock or damaged, setting you up for a laboured start.

PLANTING AND MAINTENANCE

Once you have a healthy, strong specimen of your choosing, prepare a hole that is as deep as the root ball with a little bit of broken soil underneath it. Be sure the hole is a further 30cm wider all the way around the root ball, then backfill it with soil to allow your tree a nice pit to start growing.

Once planted, protect the base of the tree with a layer of mulch, around 5–10cm deep, spanning 60cm out from the trunk. Then hammer in two strong stakes (without hitting the root ball) on either side, securing the trunk between them with a length of webbed tape. After a couple of years, once the tree has established strong roots, these stakes can be removed and the tree will continue to grow happily unsupported.

Over time, trees need to be pruned for their health and structure.

Chris recommends engaging a New Zealand Arborist Association-approved contractor to tend to the tree in its first two to three years, ensuring the tree canopy is in the best form to mature, resulting in less pruning costs in the years to come.

CHRIS'S FAVOURITES

Below: My old cherry tree has plenty of room to thrive, providing welcome shade in the height of summer plus beautiful interest with blossom in spring and autumn colour.

It's always a treat to learn from the experts, so I asked Chris to name some of his favourite trees. 'I love the *Fagus sylvatica* (copper beech) as a tree for large sections. The branch structure is dominant, and the colour is magnificent. The *Acacia baileyana* 'Purpurea' (Cootamundra wattle) is a nice, fast -growing evergreen tree for smaller sections with beautiful foliage and flowers. And you can't beat a *Sophora microphylla* (kōwhai), with its bright yellow flowers that attract native birds.'

Given the many years a tree might take to grow to useful maturity, the knee-jerk reaction of removing it without any understanding of its advantages can lead to regret.

Privacy and fences

KEEPING OUT THE NOSY NEIGHBOURS

Privacy at home in the city has been front and centre of my mind since I removed my protective belt of trees. As inappropriate as they were for my plot, they did do one job very well, and that was reducing the amount of accidental eyeballing between us and our poor neighbours.

Over the past few years, aside from my own self-directed privacy destruction, two other neighbours have removed trees on their properties that have opened up unfortunate lines of sight. I've come to realise that we are a little worse off with the traditional raised platform of our 1908 villa, peeking over your average 1.8-metre fence with ease by just glancing out the window.

We once decided to attack our towering hedge of *Griselinia littoralis*, which gave an awesome buffer between ours and the rental next door. After an hour of precarious chainsaw action at height, we stood with hands on hips staring at the half-chewed wall of green. It was painfully obvious that more regular maintenance had been needed and, as I stuck my head into its midst, I realised we had let it swallow up more than a metre of space. This beast was now more hindrance than help, and dramatically, the whole thing came down. As both the light and wider streetscape came tumbling in, I reassured myself that there were more suitable tree options to explore.

Our most successful efforts of privacy creation have all been helped along by the addition of panels of trellis along the top of the fence. A patchy and somewhat pricey option that does give a level of instant relief. Combined with climbing foliage, I see this as my optimal solution. Of course, climbing foliage comes with its own challenges, too.

When we purchased our place, immature swathes of *Ficus pumila* (creeping fig) were just getting established across our wooden front and side fences. Wooed by the romance of these greening walls, I let it run rife. I paid heed to warnings of its maturing woody arms with thick leathery leaves that start growing horizontally (as opposed to vertically),

Opposite: The dark stained fence pulls attention down from the neighbours roofs. Seen here with early spring aquilegia, Dutch irises, phlomis and young shoots of *Verbena bonariensis*.

by clipping them back hard a few times a year. After our neighbour
expressed concern that our shared fence was being damaged, we
stripped it all back to survey the issue. In all honesty, the fence beneath
was old and the ficus was barely affecting the pales, which were jumping
off the frame. As a result, it's my plan to let it regenerate but monitor
their side closely for any naughty breakthrough that might grow woody
and destructive. Above all, ficus is a plant that can grow from a narrow
strip of unloved ground, a spot many others wouldn't handle.

I needed to address my back garden borders with a little more
creative thought. After successfully employing sheets of metal
foundation grid to grow sweet peas up, we have tacked additional
sections to a problem length of fence, to have a go with a *Hardenbergia
violacea alba* (white coral pea), an evergreen climber with beautiful
flowers. Double-tick in my book!

Like lots of those fleshy, pretty climbers the risk is it maturing to
sparsely leafed foliage at the base and a big ball of chaos at the top of
the fence in the sun. I'm currently experimenting with pinning some of
its tendrils to the ground to encourage multiple new vertical shoots to
get better coverage down low. Time will tell on that one!

For our main area of concern, where the now removed trees used
to block the neighbours view into our living area, I have entered a
new realm of my gardening adventure. After previously harbouring a
mean prejudice against camellias, I have softened to appreciate their
reliability and advantages.

Previous owners had planted two *Camellia sasanqua* and attempted
to espalier them behind what would have been petite, new feijoa trees.
As the feijoas grew and smothered them, the camellias demonstrated
their outrageous hardiness by surviving with no attention for five years.
For the first time, I saw their potential as glossy evergreens with winter
blooms that could be trained to create a gentle green wall.

A further three sasanqua plants were purchased and lines of evenly spaced wire were strung tightly along the fence to help train their spread. After pouring over espalier styles, I have chosen the 'abstract' style, in which I train, with limited finesse, any available branch to spread up and wide in whatever haphazard form results!

Aside from a *Trachelospermum jasminoides* (star jasmine) that has been doing a good job on a section of fence under duress, I am also considering employing a *Rosa banksia* (Lady Bank's rose) in another space. Its evergreen nature, thornless stems and little butter-coloured blooms appeal.

With four bordering neighbours I want to keep relations happy so careful consideration will be given to its support to protect the integrity of the fence, likely employing foundation grid again.

Below: After removing a row of trees that provided privacy from our neighbours, I have planted *Camellia sasanqua* that I will train along and up the fence – eventually creating an evergreen screen.

Food or flowers?

WHY GARDENERS SHOULD BE PLANTING BOTH

In the beginning, it was the visual possibilities of gardening that captured my attention. My interest was lured away from a focus on interiors by the potential of creating beautiful, naturally powered outdoor environments.

As a former interior designer, I was keenly aware of the impact spaces could have on a person's state of well-being and my eyes were opened to the possibilities of experimenting with this outside. At first, I was led by an obsessive attraction to airy, flower-focused planting above all else, something I am happy to report is now broadened by a healthy respect for trees, shrubs, grasses and structure (page 88).

I will readily admit, however, that getting my hands in the dirt was not initially triggered by a desire to grow food. Over the years the Pinterest-worthy stacked vegetable garden that I inherited with this property has seen some pathetic attempts at vegetable planting, mostly crowded by the ornamental plants I popped in there to take

Opposite:
Raspberries in autumn glory at the Blue House in Amberley, North Canterbury.

advantage of the all-day sun the beds enjoy.

But with the ever-increasing cost of living, and the depressing monthly letters advising a rise in mortgage rates, I pulled myself together and am pleased to say that vegetables now have priority in that space. I am not, however, sacrificing the sunny spots I have reserved for dahlias and the self-seeded crop of nigella that is roving around the edges.

My entry into gardening certainly feels a little back-to-front compared to the experiences of many of my peers. In all honesty, as I delved into the local gardening community on Instagram, I noticed an underlying vibe from those whose vegetable gardens were their primary focus – dare I say it, there was a righteous tone: 'I grow food, not flowers'. It still feels misguided to me – sort of like eating cake but leaving the icing because it's not worth the effort despite the fact that, in combination, it completes the full experience.

I also found the almost evangelical preference of growing everything from seed as opposed to supplementing with the cheap and cheerful punnets from the garden centre kind of oppressive. Each to their own, of course, but surely utilising both options keeps gardening accessible in response to the demands of time and space available. In my experience, both methods will present unpredictable results, as is true with all gardening.

During the Covid lockdowns, I received regular messages from people my age excitedly reporting that they were growing flowers for the first time. Many were not beginner gardeners, but keen vegetable growers who had never dared divert any effort into something so frivolous. Yes, an ornamental flower bed might not stock your fridge, but it feeds the soul in a way that broccoli just can't.

In a casual discussion with a team member at the Christchurch Botanic Gardens, we touched on this subject, and he pointed out

Opposite above: Homegrown onions planted amid flowering plants. **Opposite below:** Romantic blossom on my dwarf apple tree planted in a barrel.

The 'one or the other' stance of growing vegetables versus ornamentals can stand in the way of building a beautiful little ecosystem.

that the exclusion of flowering plants from a garden will negatively impact crops. Beyond the obvious, that flowers attract important pollinators (page 42) to aid in the fertilisation of vegetables and fruit trees, low yields can also be a reflection of their absence.

Flowers also attract beneficial predators to your patch with the likes of ladybirds moving into nectar-rich spaces where they will feed on that annoying influx of aphids. In my own garden, I observe a lot of birdlife even over winter, likely due to my holding off on cutting back the crispy seedheads of my flowering perennials, which the birds gratefully snack on.

As a slug issue arose thanks to my efforts at mulching with pea straw, I also lamented the huge mess the blackbirds were making by scattering the messy fibres across the lawn. It didn't initially occur to me that they were dealing with my unwelcome slug population and that there was a positive to the (albeit messy) bird activity. My seedheads encouraged their residence and, as a result, I reaped the rewards.

What I am getting at here is that the 'one or the other' stance of growing vegetables versus ornamentals can stand in the way of building a beautiful little ecosystem.

On observing the planting of more mature gardeners, I certainly notice that there are always, without fail, areas provided for both food and flowers. To them, gardening isn't separated into one or the other and is certainly not deemed nobler by the exclusion of either.

So while I am inspired to plant more lettuce at the foot of my dahlias going forward, I hope that passionate vegetable gardeners might dip their trowel into growing some petals for their own pleasure, too. Gardening beyond function only might connect you more deeply with the satisfying seasonal flow offered to us by Mother Nature.

Next page: *Dahlia* 'Honka Fragile' surrounded by other ornamentals and vegetables happily sharing space in the garden.

Mix up your flower shapes

VARY BLOOMS FOR MAXIMUM INTEREST

During my initial energetic burst of enthusiasm for this whole gardening business, I bought the book *Brilliant and Wild: A garden from scratch in a year.* As if the title wasn't enticing enough, at the time the author, Lucy Bellamy, was also the editor of my favourite gardening magazine, *Gardens Illustrated*, a go-to for international gardening inspiration with a naturalistic bent.

In compiling lists of fabulous and unusual plants, she divided them into chapters based on their flowering forms, further encouraging readers to choose from each to make a richly textured garden beyond selecting based on colour alone.

I found Bellamy's breakdown very accessible, compartmentalising and making sense of what always felt like an overwhelming menu of options when curating for my own garden. Reflecting on the much-appreciated angle she offered, I started thinking about the interesting plants I have added to my garden over the years and those I have investigated with their distinctive form in mind.

While there is no escaping my personal attraction to softness in planting, I have found the addition of, in Bellamy's words, 'dots, panicles and spikes' amongst bushier specimens, offers a sense of whimsy that brings the desired informal vibe to my urban space.

With a focus on my summer and autumn perennial display, plants like echinacea, rudbeckia, helenium, Japanese anemones, scabiosa, geum and knautia have long been my favourite ways to introduce dots of colour to my beds. Their bright and bold flowers (some larger than others) float through the longer stems in the garden and provide beautiful anchors for the eye. My mysterious and unidentified self-seeded crop of asters, with their tiny mauve flowers, have been most welcome in autumn, even if the plants themselves collapse open to the ground at any given chance.

As I sought to push myself beyond what I was used to, I popped

Opposite: The extraordinary fluffy pink catkins of *Sanguisorba obtusa.* **Next page left:** The buttery spikes of *Sisyrinchium striatum* mixing with *Oenothera lindheimeri* (gaura). **Next page right:** The tiny lilac flowers of self-seeded aster that arrived in my garden.

Coreopsis verticillata 'Moonbeam' into the mix, with its delicate daisy-shaped blooms in a glowing lemon. As it shifts through autumn I also appreciate its rounded habit dotted with dark seedheads. The inclusion of a self-seeding crop of a few eryngium varieties have also added fantastical interest to my beds. Their otherworldly, prickly heads offer a playful juxtaposition to the softness around them.

More delicate in nature compared to the plants above are the array of panicle-headed options I have very much enjoyed. These are plants whose heads are made up of many tiny flowers that are read as a single bloom, throwing out their magic on slim stems. I have a particular love of tall, architectural *Verbena bonariensis* and its long flowering puffs of violet that are heavenly for butterflies. With similar tones, its lower-growing cousin *Verbena rigida* loves to weave through others closer to the ground.

Sanguisorba has perhaps been my favourite addition in the last few years, and I've experimented with two varieties. *Sanguisorba obtusa* has crazy, fluffy pink blooms that distinctly remind me of the childhood TV show *Fraggle Rock*, and my favourite, *Sanguisorba officinalis* (Great Burnet), displays a spray of small rusty bullets atop towering stems.

In early and mid-summer there is also no escaping the glory of *Thalictrum delavayi* 'Hewitt's Double'. Its scopey height and enthusiastic flowering create the illusion of lilac smoke against my dark fence. I have two other thalictrum varieties that are shorter growing with larger flowers in white and soft pink (page 238).

Then we have the spikes and spires of my garden. Perhaps the most pronounced is tough *Phlomis russeliana*, with its broad upright stems dotted with evenly spaced balls that move from acid green, to yellow petals and onto dried sculptural forms in winter. My eyes have recently been opened to the other attractive varieties of this plant, and I am now on the lookout for the pink-petaled *Phlomis tuberosa*. They

Next page: Mixing different-shaped blooms provides a richness of seasonal interest. Here I have various varieties of echinacea, *Veronica longifolia* 'Alba', *Sanguisorba officinalis*, *Scabiosa caucasica* 'Fama White', *Knautia macedonica* and *Verbena bonariensis*.

offer a weird and wonderful element planted amid more airy plants.

Thanks to some generously gifted plants, I have made the move of dotting the strong clumps of *Sisyrinchium striatum* through some other very gentle forms. With its silvery green, sword-like leaves and strong stems adorned with clusters of soft yellow flowers in late spring/early summer, it has offered further welcome interest to the mixed planting. Regular deadheading has kept the plants fresh and the flowering going, also avoiding any unwanted self-seeding.

Salvias are very popular, and rightfully so. Aside from my healthy crop of *Salvia uliginosa* (bog sage) mass planted on a bright corner, previously I hadn't had much luck in growing salvia, likely due to putting the right plant in the wrong place. But this changed with the planting of new beds where I successfully dipped my toes into this enormous genus with the introduction of bushy and tall-growing *Salvia* 'Amistad' and lower clumping *Salvia nemorosa* 'Caradonna'. Both have such deeply purple blooms they appear almost navy.

I have a romantic white veronica that has been a little challenging due to its succumbing to powdery mildew, but with each year my plants mature in size and the lovely long spires have become a valued feature at the edges of my border. Deadheading has made an enormous difference to the flowering period.

Other notable spikes and spires I have experimented with are an array of cream and pink astilbes and the wonky tops of *Lysimachia clethroides* (gooseneck loosestrife), both of which thrive in slightly shadier spots. And for some longevity and hardiness, I recommend exploring the world of penstemons, which sport large, loose spires with a storybook vibe.

When summer and autumn slide into winter, it's the seedheads and stalks of these plants that provide ghostly, structural character amid the dismal melt of the dahlias. Their extraordinary shapes enable a continued interest in the garden until I tidy it all up, ready for another season.

Umbellifers
THE DELICATE UMBRELLAS OF THE GARDEN

As a never-ever grower, learning to garden can feel like a giant undertaking. Too much to learn, too much to retain, and too much to be bothered with. But once the growing bug has a grip on you and the wins start to outweigh the misses, you will discover the total delight of curation.

Picking and choosing which plants you'd like to plough your efforts into and which specimens you want to enjoy each season is truly rewarding. Both visually and emotionally.

Looking beyond colour to also explore shape and form is where you get to experiment and discover your green-thumbed creativity. As you learn, you'll find combinations you love, appreciating plants for their foliage and blooms right through to their seedheads.

One of my favourite forms to incorporate into my garden is the 'umbellifer' – a flowering plant that belongs to the Apiaceae (celery) family. With a membership of hundreds of genera and thousands of species, these plants are broadly characterised according to their

Opposite: Armfuls of *Foeniculum vulgare* (common fennel). I am careful to avoid extensive self-seeding by harvesting the flowers or cutting the heads off before mature seeds fall to the ground.

Fennel
Astrantia
Parsley
Queen Anne's lace
& Orlaya

flowers, which develop as 'umbels' (meaning 'umbrella-like'). Bursting from the tip of a main stalk, small stems swoop upward, bearing tiny flowers that group together in a disc shape or sometimes slightly domed.

Perhaps the most common umbellifers in our New Zealand gardens are the bolting blooms of our carrot, celery, parsley, parsnip and coriander crops. Not to mention the towering heads of fennel, both within bounds and roaming riverbeds in the wild. Poisonous hemlock is in the mix there too, posing as the more lovable Queen Anne's lace (wild carrot), as are the sturdy giant heads of roadside angelica.

Below is a list of my personal favourites for the garden and the vase.

FENNEL

Fennel would be my 'gateway' umbellifer. I introduced it before I had any real recognition of the umbellifer family and, as a beginner, it quickly gave me the eager growth and blooms needed to raise my gardening confidence.

I grow the common perennial variety of *Foeniculum vulgare*, as opposed to Florence fennel, with its edible bulb. Maturing to lofty heights of nearly 2 metres with a bushy, bossy habit, I simply cut into the clump and thin it out during its most prolific growing season from spring into autumn. This allows other airy plants close by to weave through it and give the lovely wild feeling that I pursue.

With the knowledge that the plant will regenerate quickly, I harvest flowers liberally to enjoy inside. Fennel flowers are best picked when they are acid yellow/green or just forming seeds to prevent wilting in the vase. The remaining heads on the plant will develop and mature seeds that you can share with the birds, as well as harvest for your pantry.

I give my plants a strong chop back as soon as they're looking like the seeds are dropping, as I have learned from experience that they will likely get growing wherever they land!

ASTRANTIA

In great contrast to fennel, astrantia is a delightful, delicate perennial umbellifer with starry flowers that bring light and interest to partly shaded areas (page 238). Commonly maturing to around 30–60cm over lovely fern-like foliage, varieties offer flowering options in a spectrum of plums through to white with dashes of green. After a few years, I dig up and divide the clumps to create more plants with the excitement of enjoying further blooms from summer right through to late autumn.

They have a terrific vase life and truly belong in every flower bed!

PARSLEY

I know that this might be a weird one, but its inclusion here is to help you find the silver lining in your parsley bolting to flower in the heat of summer. Both my flat-leaf and curly varieties have rewarded me with terrific little umbels that look sweet in the garden as well as performing incredibly well in a vase! Perhaps don't be so quick to cut blooming heads back this season, or at the very least, add them to mixed arrangements for quirky interest.

QUEEN ANNE'S LACE (TRUE AND FALSE)

Often mistaken for each other, *Ammi majus* (false Queen Anne's lace or Bishop's flower) can be identified by its pure white, umbel bloom atop long stems and ferny foliage, whereas the *Daucus carota* (Queen Anne's lace, Dara or wild carrot) flower can appear white through to speckled burgundy, and always sports a telltale spot in the centre of its umbel to help with identification!

Both are cottage garden staples with the latter perhaps considered a little 'weedier'. Reaching up to 1.2m high with carrot-like feathery leaves, both types bring a softness to the middle or back of sunny garden beds.

ORLAYA

This is a magical, lacy umbellifer with a more boldly defined head of petals than its other cousins in this family. In New Zealand the most commonly available variety is *Orlaya grandiflora* 'White Lace' – a nod to its common name of white lace flower.

Orlaya is easily grown from seed and has a penchant for self-seeding as it comes to the end of its cycle. This enchanting annual will grow to around 75cm high if planted with space in a spot that receives good sunlight.

I thoroughly enjoy it in my garden and always have my fingers crossed for some more self-sown surprises. It is a romantic highlight within a mixed bed as much as it is in a mixed arrangement and has a very rewarding vase life for those that love picking.

Below: The magical, long-lasting flowers of astrantia. **Next page:** The dome-headed umbels of *Daucus carota* (Queen Anne's lace) with their delightful variance in colour.

Eager seeders
CELEBRATING AND LAMENTING THE KEEN SELF-SPREADERS

Spring sees a return to the time of year when the garden begs for multiple visits a day. If the sun is out, and I leave my desk or studio for a break, my normal track through the house is extended to enjoy a loop of the garden, too. There is so much to see back there and the rapid new growth charges up every part of my existence. Even the odd unseasonal sea-level snow can't stop me from grabbing at every whisper of spring!

The eager self-seeders are something to both celebrate, and lament.

As the season develops, I notice lush patches of annual *Orlaya grandiflora* pop up. Also known as white lace flower, orlaya is a gorgeous umbellifer (page 222), broader in petal than its cousins like Queen Anne's lace. From just three little plants grown from seed, the dropped seeds have been working to their own programme, with the first signs of new plant growth revealing themselves in autumn and bolstering up over winter. It was a great surprise to me given the sluggish performance of the few plants I had at first, and absolutely no

Opposite: A self-seeded sunflower joins fellow self-seeded *Verbena bonariensis* and nasturtiums in the vegetable garden.

sign of self-seeded growth until it suddenly seemed to be everywhere!

While feeling very grateful that somehow the orlaya has sorted itself out, I notice other eager self-seeding residents raising their heads, too.

Providing they were invited in the first place, self-seeding annuals are an absolute gift in my eyes. For those of us who drag our feet a little when it comes to seed-raising, the spread of beauties that return their children with little or no effort from the gardener can be something to relish.

My sweet pea spot along the sunny fence throws up new vines each spring, a continual cycle of fresh, self-generated growth that occurs like clockwork despite not introducing any new plants. Sunflowers have also been known to self-seed in my vegetable garden.

Each spring I see the sporadic patches of larkspur that try enthusiastically to flourish each year, existing now as memories of the only plants I introduced to the garden when I first started growing. I never bothered growing them on purpose again, as the powdery mildew became boring but, despite that, seeds still find space and reason to have a go. When these plants start to tinge with that all too familiar silver, I simply rip them out with little care.

Spring also sees the shadowy end of the garden welcome a carpet of rambling forget-me-nots. While they were never offered a formal invitation to the property, I find their softness and spread extremely romantic in the crisp brightness of the season. They are punctuated by islands of pink nemesia that seem to have adopted a permanent, self-directed residency in every bright nook and cranny it can find. I have thick fuzzy stands of foxgloves claiming the most awkward of spots, jamming their toes between brick paving and garden edges, but there is no way I can bring myself to pull them out.

I'm also always extremely pleased to see the early soft growth of nigella slowly reaching different parts of my borders come spring.

Next page left: I welcome the spread of softly seeding *Knautia macedonica*.
Next page right: By letting the seeds drop I get a handful of new eryngium plants each season.

It's taken tree removal and new bed establishment to finally
encourage them to take up a bright regular spot and add to the ramble
with their beautiful starry blooms.

By nature, self-seeding plants tend to make their own plans, and
these are not always in line with the gardener's. *Verbena bonariensis*
might be a slow germinator but it is ridiculously enthusiastic in
its strike rate when in the garden. On one hand, this is helpful for
replenishing my intentional planting as each established clump is
really only healthy for about three years, but it can be too much of a
good thing at times.

Equally, I love the annual arrival of my nasturtiums but they come
with so much gusto and the apparent sole aim to dominate everyone
around them. With all of these overachievers, I simply pluck out what
I don't need before their roots get really established.

In contrast, gentle self-seeding perennials like *Knautia macedonica*,
echinacea, eryngium and geum politely offer me one or two new
babies a year, and I simply wait until they are established before
plucking out and repositioning to my liking.

On the flip side, I have much less fondness for the rampantly
aggressive spread of my *Acanthus mollis* (bear's breeches), which I
have tried to banish for a few years but the seed bank is outrageous!
They are so difficult to remove with their tough, deep roots, I have
actually given up and am allowing them a somewhat controlled piece
of space. And while I love fennel in my garden, intermingled with
perennial planting, I am mostly very stern in thinning out its limbs
and immediately removing any developing seedheads. Apparently not
stern enough, however, as a tough crop is currently trying to establish
itself in an arid bit of earth and it is almost impossible to pull out with
roots intact. That's why it's a real concern when you see it growing
wild through our river beds!

By nature,
self-seeding
plants tend
to make their
own plans,
and these are
not always in
line with the
gardener's.

I have a nostalgic attachment to lemon balm, but would prefer it if it didn't want to grow everywhere! With each plant successfully pulled out, another will replace it a few weeks later. And I have really fallen out of love with my self-seeded crop of dahlias. I feel unlucky to have never received anything more interesting than a standard pink, single-petaled specimen so now simply remove any that I haven't planted myself.

There is obviously a double-edged sword to introducing any keen plant to your garden and there is a responsibility to prevent them escaping your borders. This management extends to unwelcome weeds like *Clematis vitalba* (old man's beard) that you must eradicate to prevent it spreading into delicate habitats. With my keen, less harmful garden self-seeders, I still prefer editing those back rather than giving space for swathes of foreign invading weeds.

Below: The sweet springtime show of forget-me-nots that I let ramble where they choose.

Part-shade plants

FLOWERS THAT THRIVE WITHOUT FULL SUN

As a beginner, I took the brutal course of trial-by-error when experimenting with flowering plants in my partly shady beds. Determined to replicate the rambling vibe of the abundant flower gardens I had been admiring on Instagram, I ploughed forth on planting a library of sun-loving plants in the dimly lit corners of my plot.

It took me many a mistake to connect the dots that my fence and tree-shaded beds weren't a friendly environment for most of the fun plants I wanted to grow.

Even when it looked like I might have a success, they were slim wins – bearded irises blooming but growing extremely lopsided seeking the light, peonies leafing up but never flowering (not once over three years), and my bog sage sulking like a teenager barred from its phone.

So back to the books (and internet) I went, religiously reading up on the growing conditions for every plant that caught my eye. The result is a full, flowering bed despite the lack of full sun. This is thanks to a handful of winners that coped with my testing and have thankfully proven to look beautiful mixed together.

THALICTRUM

An extraordinary late spring/summer flowering perennial that brings as much pleasure from its blooms as it does its fern-like foliage. I had such luck with my first *Thalictrum delavayi* 'Hewitt's Double' that I shot down to pick up more from the perennial sale bench at my local garden centre. I then divided my three plants to create six, and was rewarded with a towering display lighting up my semi-shaded bed. 'Hewitt's Double' grows extremely tall – around 2 metres – with at least half of that made up of misty sprays of tiny, lilac flowers that are often mistaken as gypsophila. It does need a level of staking to protect the plants from the wind, but it is a gorgeous option for picking if you can bear to remove the beauty it brings to your garden.

Opposite & next page: The fairy floss spray of flowers and towering tops of *Thalictrum delavayi* 'Hewitt's Double' in the back corner of my garden.

Thalictrum Astilbe Astrantia Solomon's seal & Phlomis

In contrast, I have also collected its close cousin, *Thalictrum delavayi* (Chinese meadow rue), which grows to 1.5 metres and has exquisite bell-shaped flowers. With a more delicate stature, *Thalictrum delavayi* 'Alba' offers creamy white blooms and a compact size.

All are terrific options in a semi-shade garden, bringing splendour with their unique blooms and foliage that you can be picking from spring.

ASTILBE

Astilbes were the first shade-tolerant plant I found with a flower that I loved. Like their perennial friends listed here, astilbes are winter dormant, retreating right back to their roots before emerging again in spring. They also divide extremely well.

Astilbes have a surprisingly wide spread of foliage from their clump, which remains until the first frosts, keeping your garden looking full. For me, the succession of flowering has been a welcome surprise with my creamy *Astilbe arendsii* 'Diamant' blooming first, followed by the candy floss pinks of *Astilbe arendsii* 'Gloria' and finishing with the taller deep pink *Astilbe chinensis* var. *taquetti* 'Lilac' in mid-summer. Their fluffy, peaked blooms then slowly fade to rust as they set seed, continuing to offer interest until the clumps start to recede in late autumn.

ASTRANTIA

I still remember the day I spotted the intricate, delicate blooms of astrantia in an arrangement and immediately went into investigation mode to find out more. A headline when hunting online described it as 'the most beautiful perennial you have never heard of' – something I couldn't agree with more!

Astrantia offers lovely, clump-forming foliage shooting up long stems with multiple flower heads. And they are truly magical, lasting an eternity on the plant as well as in a vase. Arriving in summer, astrantia

Opposite above: The creamy peaks of *Astilbe arendsii* 'Diamant', which flower late spring.
Opposite below: *Astrantia major* 'Star Bush' bringing light and delicacy to my partly shaded beds.

is generally the last plant flowering in my garden before true winter arrives. My favourites are *Astrantia major* 'Rubra', with its deep plump accents and *Astrantia major* 'Star Bush', with its green-tipped petals. I am sure my collection will grow.

SOLOMON'S SEAL

Polygonatum is an elegant addition to your partly shaded areas, with its gently arched stems that dangle creamy bells from late spring. It looks particularly good planted in drifts rather than sporadically, where it can get drowned out by bushier plants – for me, its clumps add a quieter note to my beds. Slowly spreading by rhizome, it's easy to chip at the clumps with a sharp spade if you want to reduce its spread or dig up some rhizomes to separate and plant elsewhere. Providing it is not in all-day full sun and is planted in rich soil, Solomon's seal is relatively drought hardy once established. This beautiful plant is a favourite for flower arrangers with an extremely long vase life and a romantic form.

PHLOMIS

Specifically, here I am referring to *Phlomis russeliana*, commonly known as Jerusalem sage, which is particularly gifted at 'the spread'. While it's a bother for some, I am always grateful for a plant that needs editing back as opposed to allowing space for weeds and is adept at coping with dry, partial shade.

Phlomis has a fantastical form, with broad fuzzy leaves and alien-looking flowers that dot their way up straight, rigid stems, exuding a distinctly Dr Seuss vibe! It is a nice early offering, with bold green buds forming in spring to arrive at yellow-accented blooms in late November. For me, no doubt their best attribute is the strong structure they offer the garden, remaining as a feature long after seeds have formed and offering up interest (and bird fodder) right into winter.

Opposite above: Resilient and tough, *Phlomis russeliana* provides springtime blooms and ongoing interest with their seedheads and bold foliage. It copes in both sunny and partly shady dry spaces. **Opposite below:** A stand of Solomon's seal at Flaxmere garden.

The Blu
House

Extraordinary
drought tolerant
planting of Jenny
Cooper including
Poa cita, Artemisia
'Valerie Finnis',
Verbena bonariensis
and *Sedum*
'Autumn Joy'.

WITH JENNY COOPER

Beautiful resilience

I had planned for my first visit to Jenny Cooper and Chris Raateland's garden in Amberley to be a brief one, squeezed in as a final stop in the Hurunui Garden Festival in October 2021.

I had heard the 'Blue House' murmured through the crowds over the four-day event, and on visiting, in the low, late glow of the spring dusk, I felt like screaming in delight. The incredible creative refuge I had found myself in was deserving of far more than murmured praise and a fleeting visit. Here was a garden, hidden from passers-by, that answered my long-held lust for witnessing naturalistic-style planting locally. I was instantly inspired by it and remain so ever since.

I finally found the opportunity to return and spend more time with the gardener/visionary Jenny Cooper, holding her wisdom and wit hostage until after dark. As I have come to know Jenny I've found a deep connection to her planting decisions and aesthetic. Her own journey in creating this garden was not evident to me at first, as I simply drank up the invigorating treats she offered at every corner of the property.

Opposite above: Heads of ratibida glowing in the late summer sun. **Opposite below:** Shade-loving plants are protected from the harsh North Canterbury sun.

But hiding behind the romantic result is a long journey of grit and discovery that saw Jenny bend to the environment she was creating in and learn an entirely new approach (page 166).

'My previous gardens were town gardens with fences, endless free water and established trees on around 800 square metres. I took those things for granted, as it was not until I found myself without them that I really had to sit up and take notice,' relays Jenny. 'I used to mulch and feed to the max with six inches of beautiful homemade compost every year. The garden beds would eventually rise up out of the ground and tumble forward onto the lawn because there was so much mulch.'

In 2013 Jenny and Chris purchased this bare property, all 4600 square metres (just over an acre) of it. They had arrived to an average rainfall of just 650mm per year, and the infamous heat, cold and treacherous nor'west winds of North Canterbury. They were confronted with the challenge of making a new home and garden out of a lean sheep paddock with wire fences and a single sheltering hedge on the eastern side.

In an intense demonstration of gardening being a continuous learning curve, Jenny was brutally punished for applying her formative growing approach to this unforgiving section. She took on the back-breaking work of hand-digging the beds, removing vigorous grass, working in compost, mulching with compost, staking and watering to assure her plants survival.

Her preferred palette of shade-loving plants got blown away or burnt to pieces (given the extreme lack of shelter), with the rich ground she'd created making everything too lush and too soft.

'The old way was exhausting and unrewarding,' she says. 'And yet I was vaguely aware of other gardens that survived in these harsh conditions. So began a journey of discovery which I am still on, and which is one of the most enjoyable and valuable things the garden has given me.'

Opposite above: A varied and vibrant mix of tough perennials and grasses.
Opposite below: The no-mow lawn is an annual feature of the garden.

Even now, in our regular dialogue, my mind swims at the extent of Jenny's knowledge and her ability to adopt it in the building and care of the garden we see today.

Turning to the internet and the library, she scoured the world for information on gardening in the wind and dry. She took a deep dive into horticultural research on water uptake, how to plant effective windbreaks, no-dig methods, plant nutrition, gravel gardens, bare rooting and mycorrhizal fungi. Even now, during our regular dialogue, my mind swims at the extent of her knowledge and her ability to adopt it in the building and care of the garden we see today.

Jenny and Chris undertook an enormous programme of shelter planting with seven mixed-species windbreaks fanning through the property. Trees are also dotted through all the garden beds; she learned that if you can't give a plant water, give it shade. Invested in the long game, all trees (and perennials) were planted as small as possible to ensure they adapted and grew to withstand their environment early on. Seduced by articles and photography featuring the work of Piet Oudolf, Olivier Filippi, James Golden, Charles Dowding, Dan Pearson and New

Above: In addition to Jenny's dry ornamental beds, she keeps an immaculate and thriving vegetable garden and orchard. **Next page:** Late afternoon light drifting through the pergola and patio.

Zealand's own Jo Wakelin (page 166), she became familiar with a relaxed, alternative approach to create a beautiful garden in contrast to her initial traditional ideals.

Where her former garden style was neat and tidy, the Blue House beds reflect her pursuit of planting that isn't constantly bothered by the gardener. There is a wildness, with plants left to express their natural character with little disease or need for staking. This has been achieved by ruthlessly planning and sustaining zones within her space, planting plants with similar needs together and culling the instant one doesn't cope. In taking the resource of water seriously, she is in constant pursuit of reducing her consumption and has succeeded in needing to water only half of the beds she has planted. Given the scale and abundance of her space, this is truly inspiring!

Despite this critical planning, aesthetics reign supreme and a less knowledgeable visitor wouldn't believe the science behind the creativity on display.

Where Jenny speaks about seduction, I too can relate in my own reaction to the Blue House. I chose to photograph in the magic of the late-summer gloaming, seeking to capture the sense of the place she has created. Light shimmered through the soft grasses, spiky globes and gentle washes of colour, pulling the eye through leafy frames created by the trees.

As an award-winning illustrator, Jenny's planting zones reflect her eye for colour and texture. They range from lush, glossy beds shaded by her maturing trees to wings of sun-drenched mixed perennials, gravel beds of architectural succulents and a pool of bronzing grass that shifts in the wind.

Opposite: Jenny's garden shed has storybook beauty and unmatched order.

Like all gardens, the Blue House is a work in motion that provides any visitor with a sense of calm, underpinned by the possibility that these ideas can be translated into our gardens of the future.

Bedding plants
THE DELIGHT OF 'PLUG-IN' ANNUALS

Suddenly it's summer and you look out the window and realise you never fulfilled the promise you made to yourself that you would grow some flowers this season. The thought of setting up seed trays makes you sigh, and you're not really feeling that confident about this growing thing yet anyway.

I'm here to release you from the idea that gardening is exclusively about growing from seed. I found, as I got started, that there was a real purist stance that if you were 'not germinating, you were not gardening'. I'm not here to dispute that growing from seed isn't rewarding and a super cost-effective practice, not to mention often the only way to grow interesting and hard-to-find plants. However, plugging locally grown seedlings into pots or garden beds is a pain-free alternative when the life wheel is going a bit too fast to have the time to grow from seed.

If you are new to garden centres you may find the signs referring to 'bedding' plants a bit confusing. Essentially, these are your cheap

Opposite: Cheerful antirrhinums (snapdragons) are easy and rewarding annuals to pick up as punnets of seedlings from the garden centre.

and cheerful punnets of flowering annuals – meaning their life cycle is completed in a single year. Buying punnets of healthy, strong annual seedlings meant that my success rate of getting a mature flowering plant was around ninety per cent as opposed to my often-disastrous seed-raising efforts. Obviously buying seedlings is less bang for your buck than buying seeds, but for the cost of a coffee you can dip your toe into growing flowers and with a bit of luck, they might be wildly good self-seeders that will go on to reward you in following years!

After a quick scan at my favourite local garden centres, I found that there were wide-ranging options of flowering annuals in punnets of six to nine seedlings for between $3.80 and $5. Not to mention deals on buying multiple punnets or the box lots of forty plants for $19. These are all robust seedlings that will mature and flower for you within the summer you purchase them, and if you are diligent with your deadheading, many will last until the first frost.

There are few opportunities for instant gratification in growing a flower garden, but I would say this is as close as you get!

ANTIRRHINUMS

I always grab a tray or two of the cheerful *Antirrhinum* 'Bubblegum Mix' (most likely labelled as snapdragons), which grow to around 45cm, and 'Madame Butterfly Mix', which grow to 60–75cm tall. They are satisfyingly plump and look beautiful planted tightly in the garden. They are also a fantastic cut flower, especially if you harvest when only the bottom few buds have opened.

COSMOS

For first-timers, the classic 'Sonata' variety in pinks and whites will introduce you to the joy of happy cosmos in your garden. Keep your

Opposite above: Explore the different varieties of nigella available as seedlings from the garden centre. Many will go on to self-seed and give you a show for years to come.
Opposite below: Cosmos varieties are brilliant additions to any seasonal garden!

eyes peeled for lucky finds like the cupcake or seashell varieties, not to mention 'Lemonade' and 'Pink Ice' to mix things up! I'd recommend checking labels so that you are aware of the mature sizes of the varieties you select, as they can vary greatly.

LOBELIA

You can buy this low-growing, airy little plant in a rainbow of colours and also in trailing (great for baskets and over pot edges) or upright form (great for garden edges.) My favourites are the sky blues and deep purples, which delightfully self-seed around my garden, growing in cracks and together with others in pots. If you live in a frost-free location, you might find that it continues to flower year-round.

NIGELLA

Also known as love-in-a-mist, this is a gorgeous, slightly otherwordly bloom that has the added bonus of having fascinating seedheads. Nigella is an eager self-seeder if positioned in the sun, which means you will get bang for your buck with thick crops of it popping up in seasons to come. Available in blues, whites and pinks, it is also an incredibly long-lasting flower for the vase.

PETUNIAS

Don't turn away just yet! Petunias might feel a bit old-fashioned but their froth factor and long flowering efforts have pulled them into my spotlight. Again they come in trailing and upright varieties, and I have had fun with the classic milky whites as much as the crazy saturated berry-coloured mixes. Keep an eye out for the double-petalled and striped varieties to bring some real frou-frou circus vibes to your pots and garden.

Opposite:
Old-fashioned petunias join trailing lobelia and an annual daisy – all picked up from the bedding plants table at the garden centre.

SWEET PEAS

This is my most recommended plant for beginners to grow due to their rewarding abundance of flowers, 'cut and come again' nature (page 192) and beauty. Designate a spot in the sun where you can easily access water and pile together a homemade teepee or offer a fence for the vines to clamber up. There are a myriad of varieties to choose from and I would recommend going all in by selecting a mix so you get to enjoy an array of colour. They are mostly deliciously fragrant (page 280), and if you keep up the deadheading and ample watering, they will reward you with endless flowers. Eventually, the vines will fade and I like to leave the seed pods to dry on the plant before dropping to the ground, where I hope for a self-seeded crop next season.

Opposite & above:
Explore the sweet
pea options
available at your
garden centre.
A sunny spot,
good watering and
regular harvesting
will extend their life.

Bold-bloomed perennials
CLOWNS OF THE GARDEN

I feel it's quite common for new gardeners to want to translate their interior aesthetic to their outside spaces. And if that is very monochromatic, simplified or 'Marie Kondo-esque', then they often find themselves ruling out bright flowers (if flowers are allowed at all), thinking that colour remains their archenemy even beyond their living room and wardrobe.

What I have discovered is that colour behaves really differently when produced by Mother Nature. For instance, I would never buy a red top or an orange cushion but I have come to prize my hot geums, and obsessively collect punchy rudbeckia. Somehow my garden is full of purple blooms, my longest disliked colour – I find myself in a love affair with the entire spectrum when applied to petals. Colour in the garden comes part in parcel with texture and form, adding the dimension that any good space requires to deliver that interesting, seasonal vibe.

My love for clownish echinacea, rudbeckia and now helenium still surprises me; it reveals a part of my style-psyche I didn't know existed. They are so outrageously graphic in shape and form it is an endless wonder that they are 'natural' and not in fact 3D-printed from a child's colouring book. All present prominent cone/dome-shaped centres that change as the season progresses, offering interest well beyond the demise of their petals. Each of these species is incredibly long-flowering – right into autumn – excellent for picking, and undoubtedly adds interest when dotted through airy, soft planting.

Counting up, I found I now have nine varieties of echinacea establishing themselves around the place. They are such a terrific example of a summer flowering perennial, bringing all of the advantages – steadily increasing displays every year, pleasing 'cut and come again' blooms and an abundance of seeds to collect and feed your bird population.

My own collection began with the classic pink-petaled *Echinacea*

Opposite:
The bold
graphic heads
of *Helenium*
'Waltraut'.

purpurea, the amber cone and starry shape of which really can't be beaten. The word echinacea is derived from the Greek meaning 'spiny one' in reference to sea urchins. Purpurea means 'reddish-purple' and refers to the classic lipstick tones of the common ray-shaped petals.

You will find many slightly different varieties under this species, with one of my favourites being bold 'Magnus', which sports a giant plump cone and flat fan of petals. A great place for the less confident to start is with the soft white varieties of 'Baby Swan White', 'Primadonna White' and 'Alba'. But once you catch the echinacea bug, browse around the options of *Echinacea angustifolia* and *Echinacea pallida* varieties, the latter with interesting droopy petals. Specifically, investigate varieties like 'Green Twister' for strange green and pink petals or attractive 'Mango', which is small and impossibly peach!

I have waded through years of experimenting with rudbeckia, testing both perennial and annual varieties. It's the former that has grabbed me and their brilliant performances have overtaken my expectations, resulting in deep yellow explosions throughout my garden.

A standout for me is the very tall-growing 'Irish Eyes', with its large sculptural blooms and a centre that starts as pale green and deepens to brown. I especially love my thick stand of *Rudbeckia fulgida* var. *deamii*, which is far more delicate, producing nice straight stems and delicate star-shaped blooms up to 1m high. The one I covet the most, however, is *Rudbeckia laciniata*, with its green cones and delicate yellow petals.

I have also dipped my toe into the land of heleniums. I was initially unsure of their predominately 'hot' range of colour varieties. The old me still sends a subconscious warning when considering anything orange! But the multiple plants I have (divided from just one) are impactful and abundant, flowering right through summer. They outlast every single neighbour in a vase and their petite form is great fun to dot through arrangements.

Opposite above: Uncomplicated and prolific flowering *Rudbeckia fulgida* var. *deamii*.
Opposite below: The beautiful bold cones of *Echinacea purpurea* 'Magnus' are a magnet for pollinators.

Colour in the garden comes part in parcel with texture and form, adding the dimension that any good space requires to deliver that interesting, seasonal vibe.

My chosen variety is *Helenium* 'Waltraut', which has petals that look like a tiger's skin. Others to put on your radar are 'Moerheim Beauty' and 'Lord of Flanders', with its maroon blooms.

All in all, providing you pick the perennial options, these cone flowers will bring you yearly joy. Grow from seed, make sure you give them some decent sun (although they aren't too fussy with part-shade) and get picking to bring the fun indoors, too. Not all are readily available at mainstream garden centres, so get searching – we have so many terrific independent nurseries that can send you these options and I have often struck gold when trawling online-trading platforms.

Below: I am so enamoured by echinacea I regularly collect new varieties. I'm unsure if I truly love the multi-coloured petals of *Echinacea* 'Green Twister', but it is a strong accent in the garden nonetheless.

Lastly, a wee tip for picking! Once the bloom fades in the vase, simply pluck off the spent petals and add to another arrangement as quirky 'balls'. Odd but playful for homegrown bunches.

Hardy annuals

YOUR GARDEN'S PARTY EARRINGS

Annuals are like your garden's party earrings. With their life cycle running over just a single year, this makes them a flash in the pan compared to returning perennials, but their good looks and cheer certainly make up for it.

The yearly sowing, raising, pampering and planting out can be a little too much effort for some, but for those dipping their toes into growing flowers for the first time, these are most certainly your gateway to a season of blooms, and the good vibes that go with them.

Within the world of annuals, there is a favourable group for beginners, labelled as 'hardy'. These are plants that typically can handle frosty conditions and will tolerate being sown directly in the ground, some as early as late autumn, but certainly all by early springtime. Consider this your heads-up for planning and gathering up some seeds now.

Opposite: *Nigella hispanica* 'African Bride' with its white blooms before forming magnificent seedheads.

Get creative with your choices. By all means, you can wait until fun punnets of healthy seedlings are available in the garden centres to skirt the seed raising. However, there are many independent growers and

suppliers that offer delightful, old-fashioned or rare options in seed that you won't easily find as seedlings.

When purchasing seeds, they will likely come with their own recommendations on how to plant. Each variety tends to have its own preferences of conditions, so I highly recommend some quick online research before you leap into sowing.

You have the option of getting plants started in winter, undercover in a glasshouse, propagator or sheltered warm spot out of the weather (page 62). Once your seedlings develop multiple sets of leaves, they can then be gently 'hardened off' by shifting trays into the open air during the day but back to shelter overnight, before being planted out as the season warms.

Many hardy annuals can be simply planted direct into the ground in springtime. In fact, many plants, such as nigella, zinnias, poppies, sweet peas and orlaya thrive when sown in place.

The real key to getting the best from your hardy annuals is to give them a nice sunny spot and keep on top of watering, harvesting and deadheading during their flowering period. Preventing the development of seedheads will vastly improve the distance of their display. Below are some of my personal favourites.

POPPIES

Papaver nudicaule – Iceland poppies – were one of the first flowers I ever planted. They behave as an annual in many places with hot summers, but will often attempt to over-winter and bloom again in cooler conditions. Planted en masse in a variety of peachy and white tones, their twisting long stalks and fragile petals pump up the atmosphere of any flower bed or vase.

I have also made use of some seed of *Papaver somniferum*, the breadseed poppy, from my sister, planting this tall-growing beauty in the garden mixed between perennials and other annuals. Its beautiful mauve petals unfold so gently to reveal large, albeit fleeting, blooms.

Despite the speed at which they move through their flowering period, the muted green pods on long strong stems really capture my attention. They look romantic and structural amid their softer neighbours and are a fun addition to flower arrangements.

Warning, these are the poppies you plant out of sight of the road so no one gets any ideas about thieving for their 'not-so-medicinal' values (they are also known as opium poppies) . . .

ANNUAL LUPIN

Specifically, I refer to the annual *Lupinus mutabilis* var. *cruckshankii* 'White Javelin', a slightly elusive lupin to get your hands on, but one to keep an eye out for. I have been growing this religiously after receiving some seedlings from a friend early in my gardening adventure.

This lupin is a gift to any new gardener, with its incredibly resilient behaviour, outrageous flowering period and divine scented bloom.

Simply push a seed into the ground in early spring and let it do its thing. As they are tall-growing – to over a metre – it's not a bad idea to stake for windy days. Provided you regularly harvest or deadhead its blooms, it will truly try to flower into winter.

ORLAYA

After seeing a glorious display of this pretty plant in a friend's garden, I raised some seeds and introduced the small plants into my garden. They really struggled away and never produced the show I hoped for.

Two whole seasons later I marvelled at the unexpected lush ferny stands of green foliage that had popped up all over the show in later winter. These burst into healthy huge plants of *Orlaya grandiflora* and proved to be the hero of my spring garden.

This discovery underlined orlaya's preference for being sown in place

Clockwise from above: *Lupinus mutabilis* var. *cruckshankii* 'White Javelin' is a tough annual that can be directly sown in place. It has deliciously fragrant flowers; Sweet peas commonly self-seed in my garden during the winter months; *Orlaya grandiflora* prefers to be direct planted and will self-seed at will. They have stunning pure white, bold petaled umbels; *Papaver somniferum*, known as the breadseed poppy.

MY TOP 5 HARDY ANNUALS

Poppies
Lupin
Orlaya
Nigella
& Sweet peas

and I gratefully scattered its mature seeds through the garden again before removing the spent plants in mid-summer. Its glowing white umbel blooms are worth the experiment!

NIGELLA

There are multiple varieties of this beautiful annual to explore, celebrating its interest from the flower through to seed pod. Like nearly all annuals, it prefers a sunny position, and its aggressive self-seeding may call for some thinning out!

Most commonly available in a pretty sky blue or white, also look out for the special *Nigella hispanica* 'African Bride', with its fantastic dark seed pods, and *Nigella papillosa* 'Spanish Midnight', a deeper variation of the common blue variety featuring dark purple centres.

SWEET PEAS

Sweet peas are a crowd favourite for their pretty blooms, heavenly fragrance and eager growth when positioned with full sun and offered ample water. They will reward any grower who dedicates time to brutally harvest and deadhead, removing all flowers except for buds off the vines a couple of times a week during its most prolific growing period. This will substantially lengthen its flowering potential before heat or disease claims them.

Perhaps the best thing about sweet peas is their willingness to self-seed in place. As the vines tire, I let seeds develop and crisp on the plant, allowing them to drop to the ground below. It's common to see seedlings pop their heads up in winter and provide an early and delicious spring show before the rest of the garden has got going. It's also possible to raise seeds undercover and plant out in early spring or summer as you please.

Other tough but rewarding annuals to explore are phlox, cornflowers, annual rudbeckia, stock, wallflowers, sunflowers and larkspur.

Flowers and fragrance

NOT JUST FOR HUMAN PLEASURE

It could be considered a blow to our human ego that the incredibly delightful, nose-tingling and transporting fragrances from the garden are only appealing to us by happy coincidence. After all, the complex chemical makeup of the essential oils developed in the petals of flowers is entirely focused on attracting not us, but their favourite pollinators.

Waiting until their blooms reach perfect maturity, plants will hold back their most fragrant performance for ideal fertilisation conditions. The resulting scent released into the air has two distinct purposes. The first is to specifically attract their ideal pollinator, the second is to remind their visitor of the great feed it has enjoyed, encouraging them to seek out the same variety elsewhere to complete the fertilisation cycle (page 42).

For instance, sweet apple blossom pulls in bees who feast on the delicious nectar, get covered in pollen and drunkenly head off to the next tree, bargaining for a repeat performance. Other plants, like evening primrose, release their headiest scent as night falls to attract their preferred moths, or in some countries, bats!

Of course, not all plants release attractive scents – or any at all. Every year I wondered why my shasta daisies were covered in fly poo, now I realise their unappealing smell is the reason. Like others in their ranks, such as sea holly and even some pear trees, these plants are on a slightly different smelly mission: to draw in flies as their preferred pollinator. Alternatively, plants like grasses that use airborne pollination, or others that focus on birds spreading their seed on their behalf, often have little to no fragrance.

Astonishingly, I discovered another reason for scentless plants. In the highly competitive world of rose breeding, mostly with the cut flower market in mind, the strong focus on visual impact and lasting form has seen the scent gene simply fall by the wayside. I think we can all agree a scentless rose feels like a travesty!

Opposite: My 'Blue Moon' rose offers welcome fragrance from its position in a barrel on our patio.

Once a flower is successfully pollinated it stops releasing its scent and instead focuses energy on the fertilised embryo's transformation into a seed, triggering the decline of the petals. A good reminder for gardeners wanting to cut and bring their favourites indoors is to get in quick with the snips as soon as a bloom looks mature and before the pollinators have rolled around in them.

Floral fragrance is so often tangled up in memories. I can fondly remember the intense scent of the daphne growing outside the kitchen door at my childhood home, the sweet muskiness of jasmine at the bach, and the wonder of the heavenly smelling wintersweet, which felt mismatched with its messy, twiggy-looking appearance.

Experienced gardeners can curate their garden beds for fragrance easily by visualising both the mature show of what plants will present as well as the learned knowledge of the special ones that will tickle more senses than just the eyes. For new gardeners looking to enhance their space, here are some great options to consider.

BULBS

Many bulbs pack a scented punch as well. Divine *Narcissus* 'Earlicheer' is unbeatable for my late winter garden, as are kitchen-table pots of hyacinth. Seek out scented mixed bags of jonquils (page 284) to join the spring chorus of delicious freesias, tuberose, peonies and bearded irises. Do your nose a favour and establish a little patch of lily of the valley to really reward your senses or join the New Zealand tradition of planting *Lilium regale* (Christmas lilies) for summer holiday cheer.

CLIMBERS

Make the most of a sunny fence or structure by employing varieties of climbers like honeysuckle, wisteria, clematis and jasmine. If no wall is available, rig up a teepee using sticks and plant around the base in sweet peas. While not all sweet peas are charged with fragrance, you simply can't go wrong with the divine *Lathyrus odoratus* 'High Scent'.

ANNUALS AND TENDER PERENNIALS

Interested in exploring what fragrance will really spin your wheels? Play around with planting annuals such as phlox, stock, sweet alyssum and nicotiana. Or dabble with tender perennials (that may behave like annuals in your climate) such as old-fashioned four o'clock flower and interesting chocolate cosmos. The latter's name says it all!

SHRUBS

For longevity and scale, consider attractive and sweet-smelling shrubs like lilac, viburnum, daphne, mock orange and gardenia to return to every year. Without a doubt, wildly fragrant roses are almost unrivalled options including heavily scented 'Margaret Merril', 'Gertrude Jekyll' and the Damask rose 'Madame Hardy' amongst others. For cooler climates, *Chimonanthus praecox* (wintersweet) rescues your starved senses in the darker months.

NATIVES

Our New Zealand natives have some fragrant stars within their ranks, too. I can still remember my astonishment at learning that the divine smell wafting in the hot wind on our coastal Canterbury farm was the scent of *Cordyline australis* (cabbage tree/tī kōuka) in full bloom. The flowers, leaves and resin of *Pittosporum eugenioides* (lemonwood tree/tarata) have historically have been used as a perfume by Māori.

In the North Island, *Alseuosmia macrophylla* (alseuosmia/toropapa) is famed for its sweet-smelling blooms, while the fragrant *Olearia rani* (tree daisy/heketara) releases its scent from coastal Banks Peninsula to Southland.

Knowing your narcissi

EXPLORING THE DAFFODIL KINGDOM

Aside from daisies, I wonder if the daffodil might be one of the first plants we learn to name as a child. They are hard to miss in their classic, yellow-trumpeted form and with little other competition as we creep out of winter, they never fail to catch our eye.

They arrive in charming gatherings or a sprawling sea with some varieties being deliciously ruffled, two-toned with peaches, pinks and intense tangerine notes – some virtually without scent and others impossibly fragrant. Giant heads to small clustered creatures on straight stems, thriving in the sun just in time for your weary winter eyes.

They are a beginner gardener's best friend, with most being eager, hardy and uncomplicated growers that love to multiply each season, easily transferring their cheer and promise into a bottle on the window sill.

Opposite: One of my personal favourites, *Narcissus* 'Grand Monarch'.

But, as I've come to learn, daffodils are anything but simply defined. While it is completely acceptable to broadly refer to anything

vaguely 'daffy' as a daffodil, for the passionate enthusiast they provide a world of difference in sometimes minuscule detail.

So let's break them down in the least complicated terms possible.

Daffodils and jonquils are spring-flowering perennial plants that are members of the genus Narcissus, part of the Amaryllidaceae (Amaryllis) family. Daffodil is a broad, common name that tends to refer to the larger-headed, trumpet-like, frilly, strong-hued to pastel varieties with one to two blooms per stem, but this term also encompasses all varieties. Jonquil, a word that is often used as a substitute for daffodil, is more correctly applied to delicate varieties that have small cupped, fragrant and clustered blooms of one to five yellow or white flowers per stem. Their spears of foliage are slightly rounded rather than sword-tipped.

Below: *Narcissus* '*Mount Hood*'.

To add to the mystery, all jonquils can be correctly referred to as daffodils, but not all daffodils are jonquils. However, all daffodils and jonquils can be correctly referred to as Narcissus/Narcissi.

Still with me?

I have found, too (as a relative beginner wading into this elaborate plant group), that you will often hear people using the term 'narcissus' quite specifically. In common garden land, many use it to refer to the earlier flowering, fragrant and double-petaled, clustered varieties with smaller, pale heads.

There are hundreds of species and over 32,000 cultivars of daffodil that have been defined. To try to identify and record them, the RHS (Royal Horticultural Society) created thirteen daffodil divisions, with quite specific points of recognition.

Division 1, trumpets: To qualify, they have one flower per stem and their cups must be longer than their petals.

Division 2, large-cupped: Easily confused with trumpets but with their cup being more than one-third (but not equal to) the length of their petals. One flower per stem.

Division 3, small-cupped: Cups must be no more than one-third the length of their petals, with just one flower per stem.

Division 4, doubles: Ruffled flower heads that produce one or more blooms per stem.

Division 5, triandrus: Two to six little blooms per stem, with petals slightly reflexed from the cup. They are often shorter in stature than their bigger cousins.

Division 6, cyclamineus: Those terrific smaller daffodils that have just one flower per stem but the petals flare sharply backward from the cup.

Division 7, jonquilla: Fragrant, with three or more blooms per stem, commonly only in yellow or white. Their leaves are distinctly different to other daffodil varieties, being tube-like with rounded tips. This is the group that can be truly specified as jonquils if you want to get techy!

Division 8, tazetta: Have a stout stem and clusters of three to twenty fragrant flowers. As a beginner, I find these can easily be confused with jonquilla.

Division 9, poeticus: Typically have white petals and cups with green/yellow centres, rimmed in red.

The remaining four divisions collect together wild forms and hybrids, split-cupped species and those specified only by their botanical names. To add some complexity (!) to the mix, there are often sub-divisions within each class above.

As a beginner, perhaps this is really far more than you need to know. Then again, understanding your favourite plants will only make them more appealing.

Early spring is the best time of year to scan around and witness the blooming of daffodils far and wide. Don't be shy to ask others about variety names so that you can collect up a list for bulb orders next autumn. And maybe satisfy your learning by googling which division these plants fall under.

In caring for your existing daffodil friends, you may already know that the best practice is to leave foliage to die back naturally after flowering. This can look messy, but resist the urge to cut or even braid the leaves together as the photosynthesis that occurs is vital to the bulb's health going into its next flowering season. Wait until the leaves are yellow before cutting them back.

Daffodils are also a total delight to pick! Due to their very sappy stems, you are best to place harvested stems in a vessel of water separately from other gathered stems to allow their sap to dispel and the cut to seal before adding to an arrangement. This will avoid them poisoning the vase water and reducing the life of the other flowers.

If the world of daffodils intrigues you and you're hungry for more, you will not only find a vast array of websites dedicated to the divisions, but also daffodil societies that are spread throughout the country. To attend a daffodil show is truly something special!

Below:
Narcissus
'Tête-à-tête'.

Blossom

REVEALING THE
WORLD OF PRUNUS

I feel so greedy in early spring, sucking up every tiny offering that my garden and surrounds have to offer. By late spring I am spoilt with so much eye candy that I don't ever pay quite the same attention as I do with my hungry winter-weary eyes.

After the barren winter months, every budding daffodil is cheered on and I happily lose time watching the tiny wax-eyes flit and swing through my first plum blossom. I welcome the white polka dots of fallen petals on my lawn and can't drive anywhere without seeking out flashes of juicy pink magnolias and sunny wattle in other people's gardens.

When visiting beautiful Banks Peninsula in those early spring months it is impossible to miss the energetic acid tinge of new growth in the paddocks or the scraggly blossoming roadside wild prunus that goes unnoticed for the rest of the year.

Aside from lamb gangs racing along fence lines, blossoming trees are surely the number one unavoidable signal that the seasons are moving forward. Even for a non-gardener, clouds of blossom amid the evergreen and spindly winter landscapes cannot be ignored, and immediately lifts the spirits out of the cool-weather hangover.

When I started gardening, the term 'prunus' conjured question marks in my mind. With better understanding now, I realise it is the easy way to refer to fruiting trees and shrubs, given it is such an enormous genus and often hard to individually identify species. Mostly found in temperate regions around the world, these plants issue clusters of white and pink flowers whose resulting fruit can be used for food. However, there are many ornamental varieties that fruit as well, but sporadically, with small inedible (to humans) offerings that nevertheless get greedily munched up by birds.

Opposite: Rows of glorious blossom in an orchard outside Little River, Banks Peninsula.

At this time of year, it is these ornamental 'wild' varieties that drag our attention to the roadsides where they have been spread over time by birds, many continuing to establish themselves through suckering.

These early-flowering species, such as the very common cherry plum *Prunus cerasifera*, hot pink *Prunus campanulata* and clustered white Japanese hill cherry *Prunus serrulata* are even listed on our national weed databases in New Zealand as naughty invaders that enter habitats without asking.

In my own garden, I inherited a number of prunus. Four ornamental cherries that seem to have no rhyme or reason with their blossoming schedule, constantly budding up ready to have another go three or more times a year! The very spiky old plum with purple foliage and pink blossom is missed now as it was diseased and had to be removed, but its cousins, bearing pretty unappetising, very messy fruit, live on for now – however I think my neighbour is hoping at least one will be banished!

I have a dwarf apple tree called 'Blush Babe' growing in a barrel that I hope will offer us twenty or so morsels if I can keep the bugs at bay, but it is a very pretty addition nonetheless.

My favourite, however, is the huge old cherry in the centre of the garden. Its dense clusters of blossom resemble giant popcorn, and only offer a few handfuls of edible cherries each year – if we are lucky.

I think the staggered flowering of prunus is their most appealing attribute. The gutsy early ornamentals make way for beautiful almond, apricot, plum and sweet cherries, then pear, apple, quince and medlars, among so many more. Up until recently, I had staked apple blossom as my favourite of them all. So romantic with the wash of watercolour pink at their centre, but then I met quince, with its incredible scent and bright green rounded leaves, and I was swayed to crown it the prettiest of them all.

The romance of blossom is celebrated through art and culture around the world. Here in Christchurch, North Hagley Park sports an avenue of the hybrid Yoshino cherry *Prunus* x *yedoenis* that draws crowds of appreciators in spring – not unlike the celebratory migration of

Opposite: Wild roadside prunus. **Next page left:** An old prunus and her decrepit friend on Banks Peninsula. **Next page right:** Blossom signals spring, but also new life and potential.

blossom watchers for the Hanami festival in Japan. This is a centuries-old custom of enjoying the fleeting and transient beauty of flowers, namely the sakura (cherry) and less often, plum. The tradition is so entrenched in their culture that there is even a blossom forecast announced each year to allow citizens to plan their gatherings when the trees are at their most abundant.

Blossom signals spring, but also new life and potential. When we speak of a person 'blossoming', we refer to a kind of revival, confidence or emerging beauty of their being. A blossoming relationship speaks of a positive and growing connection. All in all, blossom in its physical and metaphorical forms is loaded with good feeling, and is part of Mother Nature's life cycle, which drags us forward no matter what the world is doing around us.

SECTION FOUR

The encha garde

nting

In the following pages I explore the more emotionally led aspects of gardening – the ability of my garden to forgive a lack of attention at times, and the refuge it offers when the outside world feels tough.

Plants and garden spaces are able to imbed themselves in both our own stories and in the values of societies over centuries. Seeing your gardening as an enriching process rather than just a pretty outcome allows you to appreciate the hours spent in your own little piece of earth.

THE ENCHANTING GARDEN

THIS WAY, COME

A curtain billows
letting in a draught of fresh air,
inviting a glimpse of what lies outside.

There is no singular view of anything,
no one way to get things done,
no right way to live a life.

But at times your life will show itself
arriving in the dancing sunlight,
landing with a soft stirring of air.

– Mary Walker

Your garden, your way

AN UNBRIDLED PERSONAL EXPRESSION

During one early summer I held an open day in my urban Christchurch garden. This was less about presenting a pristine example of ornamental planting (something that is virtually out of reach as I am too good at turning a blind eye to the problem areas) and more about demonstrating the satisfying and rapid results of utilising perennials. I was so surprised at the fullness of some newly established beds in their first season that I wanted to share them as an encouraging example for others who might be finding the development of a garden a tad tedious.

The day went well, with five interested groups booking in for fifty-five minutes of garden immersion. Due to my loquacious ways, the visitors had no time to themselves, instead receiving a blow-by-blow report of every inch and every plant involved in my journey thus far. On reflection, I have a lot of tweaks to make in regard to my delivery – and I'm sure a cup of tea would have been appreciated!

I found it fascinating though, in the brief moments when my visitors could squeeze in a comment or a question, to see the planting through their eyes. Observations were made about the absence of rhododendrons, azaleas and an obvious lack of roses. I had to admit that I was too greedy with my small amount of ground to give those larger shrubs the room they needed and the lack of roses boiled down to a similar issue. Despite wanting to, essentially I wasn't willing to sacrifice any of my existing plant specimens to allow them space in a suitable spot!

One keen-eyed (or -nosed) visitor asked what I had planted for fragrance. This had me spinning and scanning to offer her examples, only to realise that my summer garden wasn't smelly at all! How did that happen?

Concerns were raised about my inclusion of certain plants. These warnings were absolutely fair, and I was aware of them when making

Opposite: Open garden guests exploring my early summer beds leading into Christmas.

the decision to plant. The worries were mostly centred on rampant creatures like Japanese anemones, the eager spreader *Lysimachia clethroides* (gooseneck loosestrife) and my mention of a certain hard-to-obtain lupin.

I reassured my visitors immediately that, in my space, for some reason, the anemones don't spread without me forcing them to, and that the loosestrife's eagerness was a welcome gap filler and it was very easily pulled out from the roots in one tug if needed. What's more, the lupin – *Lupinus mutabilis* var. *cruckshankii* 'White Javelin' – possessed none of the invasive behaviour of its perennial cousin the Russell lupin, and had never once self-seeded.

My plant-based decision-making was again brought to the fore after visiting the garden of a friend. I deeply admire her curation and diversity in planting, which I very well know rests on intensive research and understanding of her environment.

With the memory of her place fresh in my mind, I returned home and gazed across my own plot. The new planting I had so painstakingly planned looked impressive in its first-year fullness, tinged with a kind of chaotic fairyland appeal. Knowing each plant intimately, I hadn't stepped back to view the beds as a single entity and on doing so realised a couple of things – I seem to be obsessively drawn to airy, dotty plants, and this summer space really could be all too saccharine and busy for many people.

Had I missed my opportunity to balance the wildness with some stronger, anchoring shapes beyond my wee topiary balls that had long since been swallowed up? How is it that a former hater of purple has ended up with so much of it? And what is with all the white?

I plodded to my swinging seat under the cherry tree to consider the beds from a different angle and take in the other areas of the garden. It's here that I reflected on the journey that had led me to now.

The purchase of this property in 2017 and the tentative steps made in introducing plants that I didn't know the names of, let alone how to grow. The rising fascination and addiction to all things garden-related. The endless googling, YouTube watching, blog reading, research and book-buying followed by my own book writing and column-conjuring.

Beyond the undeniable benefits that I found for myself with those hours spent in the earth, planting, visualising and generally shutting out the entire world, I think it's the creativity of it all that hooked me.

My frothy fairy garden is as tangible a creation as the artwork I make in my studio. Each planting decision and combination (white, purple or neon peach) is my mind running away with itself in the same way I decide to combine colours in a painting. The research required on appropriate plants to reach my vision is the same as the time I spend gleaning product information from the art-store owner. The shifting of plants and introduction of new ones is the same as revisiting a painting after sleeping on it, knowing a better result is within reach.

And in the true vein of creativity, my fleeting garden canvas holds as much importance as the gardens made by each neighbour down my street. It's here that our uniquely personal values and inclinations can be expressed via Mother Nature. No art school or permission is needed.

Next page left: The soft fans of *Miscanthus sinensus* 'Morning Light' take the spotlight in autumn. **Next page right:** *Oenothera lindheimeri* (gaura) captures the attention of a bee.

The sacrifice of fragrance and dismissal of trusty common plants speaks entirely of my predisposition to lean toward whimsy and the immense satisfaction I find in visual results. 'Eager' plants are welcomed as I place more value in their appearance than in the time spent controlling them. In saying that, I still can't explain how I have become a purple person.

Houseplants
ARE THEY YOUR GATEWAY TO GROWING OUTDOORS?

The positive effects on daily life bought about by introducing nature into living spaces cannot be disputed. Sure, many people may have launched into houseplant land spurred on by the very aspirational interiors dripping in plants that whizz past them on social media and magazines, however, this doesn't diminish the goodness they bring. In fact, the mainstream garden world could only dream of riding the crest of this global trend!

If we ignore for a moment the ridiculous prices some plants have sold for in the recent past, indoor plants mostly owe their popularity to their accessibility. Your first can be bought at a hardware store for around $20 and then there is the perk of choosing a pretty pot to house it in. Bringing it home and styling it on a shelf secures the instant visual gratification that many have come to expect. The only thing required from there is to keep that single plant alive.

Buoyed by the success in maintaining this living thing, our beginner plant owner will thirst for more, drinking up the lush effect these

Opposite: Plotted plants take their spot on a locker in my kitchen.

purchases have on their home spaces. They may start increasing their budget as they eye up more exotic finds, but awareness of their plants' needs – and the time spent on care – will grow too.

Inadvertently they are connecting themselves to the natural world and building a knowledge base that won't be forgotten.

Houseplants allow people of all ages to be responsible for some 'life', albeit of the botanical kind. This act of caring for something beyond themselves is of real value to their general well-being.

Transiency comes with youth but also with renting, and with the horrific state of our property sector; for many people locked out of homeownership, indoor plants offer a welcome and achievable foray into growing. The expense of ploughing time and money into the garden of a rented home is only attractive to those with a drive

Below: A small houseplant brings nature into my hall.

to establish a garden outdoors, something that isn't as common for younger people now as it was for the generations before.

So, when would this passion for indoor growing possibly migrate outdoors? I believe this moment rests in a magical collision of age vs space vs living situation. This was certainly the case for me.

Over three years in my early thirties I grew a pretty decent collection of indoor plants that enjoyed life in my sunny Auckland apartment. On moving south again, they were all carefully loaded into the car to travel to a whole new island, landing in my newly rented home in Christchurch. Even though there was a small courtyard garden at this property and I struggled to keep my outdoor herbs alive, it was indoors that my well-travelled plant friends continued to thrive.

It was in early 2017 that we stepped through the back doors of our newly purchased home, shrewdly scanning the garden that came with it. Despite living in many rented houses with gardens over the previous sixteen years, I had never owned my own, and on reflection, this was a massive turning point for my gardening adventure.

My interest in personality-driven interiors, resting on my basic growing skills acquired from being a houseplant mother, surprisingly helped me view this new outdoor space with fresh interest.

Here was an outside room that I could experiment in, choosing beautiful plants that were never suited to the indoors. Varieties that would provide me with flowers, food and the atmosphere that I craved. It was home ownership combined with space that blew the lid off an interest I had never had before.

For those of you enjoying your rapid fall into houseplant heaven, please know that the earth outside awaits. That when your time or opportunity arrives, you can expect to be surprised that here lies an awesome source of satisfaction and beauty that your houseplanting years will put you in good stead to explore.

Garden friends

THE GREEN-THUMBED GEEKS I NEVER KNEW I NEEDED

The emergence of garden friends in my life has been an incredibly rewarding surprise.

On moving back to Christchurch in my mid-thirties, I felt very satisfied with my treasured friendship circle scattered across the country, and felt no desire to rush out to better populate my new local one. When I fell into this gardening adventure, I quickly realised my growing obsession wasn't of much relevance to most of my regulars, so it was my mum and sister who bore the brunt of the endless questions, musings and need to discuss!

As my hunger for plant-based knowledge and conversation grew, so too did the web of people I was exposed to. Garden visits, festivals and social media plugged me directly into a scene that I previously knew little about. And just like a web, each new connection led to another, until one day it dawned on me that my most regular communication was with an entirely fresh group of people. They had quite literally grown out of my garden and challenged my preconceived notions of

Opposite: My sister foraging for seeds to propagate for her own garden.

what friendship could be, and who it was with.

I have found my garden friends, more than any others, barge through peer groups and generational divides. One day I was bouncing emails back and forth for an upcoming garden-focused road trip with my best garden friends, ranging in age from their fifties to their eighties.

Our itinerary of visits and possible nursery stopovers provoked exclamations of glee in each reply, combined with plans for car-passenger swapping so we could all learn from each other while on the road. They are the garden geeks I never knew I would one day crave.

It could be mistaken that these women take on a motherly role for me, but no – our relationships are knitted in the earth, and the gossip around our favourite topic is no different to the chatter I share with my closest girlfriends, it simply has a different focus.

Garden friends are those who eagerly await an invitation to see your meagre little patch, with zero care if it's as grand as their own. The ones who explore your garden at a creep, taking in each specimen, asking for seeds, cuttings or a division when you have the time. They share their knowledge freely, sprinkling ideas and encouragement into every conversation, gently correcting you as you repeat a species name out loud for the first time!

Garden friends can easily understand your vision via verbal delivery and gain an immediate mental picture based on the plants you recite. They'll drag hoses around the lawn to draw imagined new borders and send links to their latest favourite garden websites. They constantly boost your own excitement with theirs, as this nature-based creativity is what spins their wheels, too.

Gardening has also created a bridge to my older connections, as I discovered at a lovely garden tour in Hurunui, North Canterbury, my childhood stomping ground. At each garden visited I stumbled across friendly faces from the past, parents of friends or friends of my parents. They greeted me with a different vigour, eager to chat about my column or wander the spaces together sharing our planty observations. We were crossing paths in a new way, finding delight in a shared interest as adults, not simply from former social circles.

I have found, too, that existing friendships forged over the years have been refreshed by the garden. As long-time friends find their way to gardening, our relationships have expanded to meet there. Where our conversations are still about weekend plans and who is bringing the wine, they are now longer, to fit in a two-and-fro on what is happening in the ground outside. Home visits have moved from the sofa to the backyard, where we can pick each other's brains and troubleshoot our plants together. I'd never have guessed this would be in my future.

As my garden grows, it becomes a physical record of these valued

Below: From left Jenny Cooper and Penny Zino join Karen Rhind to explore her Cromwell garden.

human connections, reflected in the gifted plants and the advice absorbed. This is proven in the fact that my bulky, unattractive camellia wasn't pulled out and instead limbed up into a trendy multi-trunked tree thanks to Jenny's advice. The shortlist for my new rose garden is strong thanks to the knowledge shared by commercial grower Claire. The inspiration to push the boundaries of my planting combinations is fuelled by Jill. The hard-to-find *Stipa gigantea* grass and *Dierama pulcherrimum* growing to maturity will forever remind me of the hours spent with Penny and the minute I wonder if I am 'doing it right' I'm reminded of Robyn's encouragement to just do it any way I want.

The support from and gratitude I hold for my garden friends is enormous, and I can only encourage other new gardeners to open up the friendship gates and find their earthy people, too.

Below: Penny Zino and Robyn Kilty examine Robyn's fabulous creative planting in Christchurch.

I have found my garden friends, more than any others, barge through peer groups or generational divides.

Tuning into the seasons

GROUNDING YOUR LIFE IN MOTHER NATURE

It wasn't until we inched out of our first nationwide lockdown for the Covid-19 pandemic in 2020 that I realised, while homebound, that I had witnessed nearly an entire single season occur in my backyard.

During this time, photo-taking became a welcome distraction to relieve the initial anxiety, secondary procrastination and general halting of normal daily routine. The process of wandering with my camera, and frankly, quite indulgent documenting of my garden each day, mainlined me into the slow but steady shift of autumn. For the first time, I noticed every change.

We began with the very balmy first half of level 4 in March, which involved beanbag reading in the sunshine, then graduated to jackets and hats for walks around the block by late April and May – autumn in New Zealand. The lack of busy life stuff allowed time and space to notice the work Mother Nature was getting up to as per usual.

I appreciated my determined cosmos and lupins refusing to give up, and my dahlias eventually throwing their last blooms before they began

Opposite: Our little Japanese maple flaming through its autumn crescendo.

their ragged meltdown ready for winter dormancy. The intense crescendo of autumn colour from our little Japanese maple was impossible to ignore – so impressive it caused us to move its wine-barrel pot to a position that we could easily see from the living room. Its last show took place with a flaming chorus that lasted a week before it dramatically dropped all its leaves in just days, forming a rusty pool on the ground.

My experiments in gardening have reconnected me to all the lovely, slow-moving signals we get that the next season is on the way, but for non-gardeners, I feel that autumn provides the easiest opportunity to plug into the ebb and flow of nature. You don't need your own garden to find comfort in the reassuring march forward that the seasons offer. Adopting a deciduous tree, a neighbour's front garden or a local park that you can easily note changes in while going about your daily business

might provide you with a steadying touchpoint. A signal that, regardless of what is going on in your world right now, there are unstoppable forces that move on despite it all, carrying you with them.

From my office window at home in suburban Christchurch I have a front-and-centre view of my neighbour's old apple tree. It gets a lot of my attention, mostly due to procrastination, but every so often I'll get a shock when I notice its seasonal development. Suddenly I'll notice it nicely ripening a generous haul of glossy red fruit, finding myself comparing its crop to previous years. I watch the birds feasting for breakfast, lunch and dinner and, once again, wonder why-oh-why my neighbours never harvest the apples for themselves. Then I witness its slow loss of leaves, revealing the gnarly old limbs and drastically unveiling the direct line of sight from their living room window into our kitchen.

My annoyance disappears as its gorgeous spring blossom arrives, coming in later than the plums and cherry trees in my own garden, but I always think it's the most beautiful. The verdant leaf growth of early summer that follows restores our privacy once again and I observe with intrigue as those tiny little green balls begin their fattening up, as is demanded every year.

This tree anchors me to the bigger picture and lifts my head back into the world when I find myself navel-gazing. I'd hazard a guess it has been doing its same routine for longer than I have been accruing birthdays and I truly find comfort and calm in noting that fact.

There are screeds of studies and books dedicated to the proven benefits of connecting with nature, but I don't believe that it has to be done in an intensive or hands-on way. Finding your own apple tree or patch of planting will open you up to the positive, soothing effect of stepping out of your life and into the moment. Not thinking about your finances, your friends and family, scary politics, global pandemics or global warming – just about the natural world silently holding it all together.

Opposite: My neighbour's apple tree. **Next page:** My husband, T, enjoying the beauty of a mild autumn afternoon in our garden.

My experiments in gardening have reconnected me to all the lovely, slow-moving signals we get that the next season is on the way.

A
VISIT
TO...

Gilroy nurseri

Glowing rose petals at Gilroy Nurseries in Clarkville, North Canterbury.

WITH
CLAIRE &
TOM GILROY

Coming up roses

In the language of flowers, roses of different colours present different meanings. To touch on just a few, white symbolises eternal love and innocence; red, beauty and desire; pink, confidence and gratitude. Overall, roses are associated with love, hope and passion, something I think we can all get behind.

It's common for gardeners to collect roses that have been bred and named to commemorate people and events, or simply to plant one as a personal symbol of remembrance or celebration. And make no mistake, the world of roses is complex and wide-ranging, littered with mind-boggling labels like heritage, floribunda, hybrid-tea, carpet, miniature, standard, bush, patio, climber and David Austin to really force some research out of you! All in all, roses are both enticing and mysterious to me as I stand near the beginning of my gardening adventure.

Opposite: Rows and rows of roses grown for garden centres nationwide.

Determined to learn more, I greedily took up the invitation to visit family-owned Gilroy Nurseries on the fertile flats of Clarkville, just

Above: Rose grower Claire Gilroy. **Next page:** Sheltered and happy, the plots of roses were like a movie set.

north of Christchurch. On a magical, still autumn afternoon, Claire Gilroy greeted me as I arrived – bucket in hand, secateurs at her hip, and sporting some seriously superior-looking gardening gloves.

We set off down a lane, bordered on one side by tall planted shelter (to deal with the charming Canterbury nor'wester) and on the other, a wild, lush block of non-flowering roses that are grown to form rootstock. From there we viewed the low, rigid rows of young plants, their glossy tufts of grafted growth showing the promise of what will be arriving in garden centres in the future.

Walking through a gate between soaring thick hedges, 'rose heaven' was then revealed. It was such a beautiful spectacle in the low golden light that I was stopped in my tracks, speechless for a moment. Tightly planted rows of blooming roses marched away from me, punctuated with petals covering the spectrum of the rainbow. It was practically a movie set in its idealistic format and, as we wandered, I was stunned at the enormous variety of shape, tone and fragrance that the Gilroys have selected to share.

As we walked the rows, stopping to admire and snip samples of Claire's favourites, I could only think about the grim, unkempt row of white icebergs at my front door, and how unadventurous they were when there was such a universe of choice available to me.

It was also fascinating to learn about the process of farming these specimens, which was framed in brutal example by Tom Gilroy working down the rows armed with a hedge trimmer!

With the aim of supplying garden centres around the country with plants in time for New Zealand's Mother's Day, preparation requires each bush to be deeply pruned back ready for transport and in a condition to be popped into their new garden homes. I wondered if the Gilroys felt sentimental knowing their plant babies were to become seasonally loved additions to gardens of all shapes and sizes. I certainly did . . .

As my eyes goggled at the vast potential of the rapidly filling bucket that Claire carried, I quizzed her on what general rose advice she could offer others like me – interested, but with little idea.

She reassured me not to be intimidated by growing roses, and that a little homework will provide huge rewards. She suggested you research to select a position in the garden that suits the type of rose you have purchased, taking into account soil preparation, access to water and the need for a sunny spot that receives a minimum of five hours of sunshine a day. We are spoilt for choice with rose varieties and they all have different attributes, both positive and negative.

Claire recommended tapping into local knowledge like your area's rose society Facebook page to learn about specific varieties that thrive in your region, a terrific idea as gardening enthusiasts will fall over themselves to help and share with newcomers. That's

just the nature of the whole gardening scene.

I left Gilroy Nurseries as the light left too, feeling outrageously inspired to explore the potential of bringing more roses into my own small, urban garden. Also, relishing the opportunity to see the work undertaken by a local flower grower who allows us those options to play.

Next time you are in a garden centre, take a moment to notice the names on the plastic plant pots, knowing that they have been lovingly grown on small farms all over the country.

Local really is lovely.

PICKS OF THE BUNCH

Below is a list of some of the Gilroys' favourite roses. Many are available across the world.

Fragrance: 'Desdemona', 'Double Delight', 'Jacqueline du Pre', 'Pope John Paul II', 'Wollerton Old Hall', 'Mum in a Million', 'Gertrude Jekyll'.

Old Fashioned: 'Mutabilis' and 'General Gallieni' – both are unique in colour and very hardy, flowering all season.

Rugosa: 'Roseraie de l'Hay' – striking colour, fragrant, hardy and good for hedging.

Rosehips: *Rosa rugosa* 'Scabrosa' – a healthy plant with immense orange-red rosehips.

Climber: 'Pierre de Ronsard' (aka 'Eden Rose') – fabulous colour, extremely healthy and has stood the test of time.

Claire's favourite: 'Ali Mau' (aka 'Duchess of Cornwall' / 'Chippendale') – it ticks many boxes with its beautiful shape, colour, fragrance, high health and excellent vase life.

Tom's favourite: 'Pegasus Bay' (aka 'Royden') – it has a vigorous healthy habit with powerful fragrance and creamy yellow flowers.

Overall, roses are associated with love, hope and passion, something I think we can all get behind.

Opposite: A 'Mutabilis' rose in the late day's sun. Above: A bucket of goodies I was kindly given to take home and arrange.

The promise of buds

MOMENTUM GAINED BY NATURE

As a pretty fresh gardener in the grand scheme of things, I am surprised that my enthusiasm hasn't waned.

In all honesty, I have a track record of launching into projects and applying myself solidly for a good two years, then moving on to the next thing. The opposite is happening to me when it comes to my garden and I know any experienced grower out there reading this will be nodding their head in understanding. I have found it to be true that with every success my gardening adventure awards me, immediately I wade deeper into an obsession that I'll likely never emerge from.

I surprised myself mid-garden wander one summer morning (my second of the day) where I eyeballed the progress of my rudbeckia, echinacea, poppies, salvia, snapdragons, scabiosa and dahlias amongst others.

I got up close and personal with their weird and wonderful buds, whispering sweet nothings and muttering that they were 'much earlier this year'. I imagined zooming out to a bird's eye view of this red-haired 39-year-old stalking her backyard in a botanic trance – and was immediately slightly weirded out!

It felt odd to recognise that my years of feverish research and experimentation have now given me a base of reference to regard the seasonal behaviour of my own wee patch. How amazing that I, a former non-grower, even have an inkling about my dahlias' normal schedule.

At the risk of sounding overly soppy, my monitoring of these beautiful strange buds marks another milestone in what has been a wholly surprising journey.

With less tripping over the basics of growing, I now have time to notice the detail. I'm no longer only in the pursuit of arriving at the 'main show' at the height of summer. Instead, I find myself marvelling at each day's changes and each season's quirks.

It quite frankly astounds me that on one day I can admire the alien

Opposite: *Geum chiloense* 'Mrs Bradshaw' with its attractive buds and blooms in springtime.

These buds promise action - not a guaranteed result, but a forward motion that's motivating in a way I didn't expect.

heads of my poppies cracking to reveal a hint of crimson silk, only to reveal their full tulle blooms the next. The glossy drops of dahlia buds still developing beside their sisters who are in full relationship with pollinators give such promise.

I am a sucker for the arrival of a new year and the delicious potential it holds with the click-over of the calendar, but I feel equally buoyed by the annual arrival of my 'bud season'. It's a period that feels like being at a pre-drinks event, getting ready for the great party to come.

These buds promise action – not a guaranteed result, but a forward motion that's motivating in a way I didn't expect. It signals that I managed to grow something, a simple joy in itself, but also reminds me that no party or project is immediate and the process is, of course, where the subtle, but equally lovely, work happens.

Below: The virgorous spikes of an echinacea bud reach for the sky between the long stalks of fennel.

Above: A dahlia
bud and bloom.
Opposite: The
early stages of
Scabiosa caucasica
'Fama White'.

The language of plants

TRADITIONS & MESSAGES FROM THE GARDEN

While on holiday a few years ago, I arrived at a tragic gap in my book lineup, where I was finished with my book but my companions weren't quite ready to share their own options! Luck saved the day, with my friend digging out a bonus book from her bag. I greedily lapped it up.

The book, by American writer Vanessa Diffenbaugh, was called *The Language of Flowers* and it centred on a fragile young woman who had adopted the Victorian system of communicating her thoughts and feelings by symbolically combining specific flowers in bouquets. It was a terrific story and I was instantly gripped by the romanticism of this secret language, immediately ordering two new books online to learn more about it.

People have given plants symbolic worth used to represent places, traditions and cultural values. Nations and regions of the world have emblematic flowers and plants, as do Scottish clans, certain religions and the Greek gods and goddesses. There are flowers assigned to align with and represent birth dates and zodiac signs, and to mark various anniversaries that might occur over a lifetime.

In Māoritanga, the tī kōuka (cabbage tree) is a signal of independence while harakeke (flax), with its strong outside leaves and fresh central growth, represents parents and their children. Respected, important leaders are compared to the great tōtara tree, while ongaonga (a type of tree nettle) might be used to describe a difficult or 'prickly' person (as shared by Te Ahukaramū Charles Royal in *Te Waonui a Tāne - forest mythology*, Te Ara – the Encyclopedia of New Zealand).

In China there is a system of messaging based on how many roses are gifted or positioned in a vase for display. A single rose signifies 'you are my only love', while eight stems says 'let us make

Opposite: In Victorian England small posies called 'tussie-mussies' were given as 'talking bouquets' to communicate messages of love.

up' – and seventy-seven is a proposal of marriage! Although not native to India, marigolds are incredibly important in Hindu celebrations. When used during weddings they represent the sun, channelling brightness and positive energy. All in all, plants allow humankind to communicate outside of spoken language.

As we well know, the natural world offers many powerful healing properties. In many cultures, however, folklore assigns more mystical advantages to different plants – and sometimes these vary quite significantly from place to place. For example, in Malta and Italy the chrysanthemum is considered bad luck when brought into the house, while in China it is thought to bring happiness. Other cultures around the world believe that wearing a gilded oriental poppy seedhead will attract wealth, while popping a pod under your pillow can bring on dreams that may answer life questions. Making a wish on the first violet of the season will guarantee it comes true, and carrying or wearing a violet will protect against bad spirits. The examples are intriguing and endless!

In nineteenth-century Victorian England, the very poised and private society got entirely swept up in the notion of unspoken messaging, instilling detailed meaning and sentiment to the combinations of flowers given or worn. Small posies, commonly known as 'tussie-mussies', were popular at this time, and were used as 'talking bouquets' – they offered silently delivered but multi-layered messages when gifted or paraded. Entire dictionaries were devoted to the complex language of flowers, known as floriography, often with conflicting information. This led to constant miscommunication, no doubt – jilted lovers at every turn!

For example, a combination of peonies, feverfew and sage could be used to send wishes of good health to the recipient. However, an individual peony can also represent romance, female fertility, wealth and hope for a good marriage. When investigating further, the common peony nods at unrealised desires, anger, shame, life and loyalty amongst many other things. I'd go as far to conclude that bouquets are probably best sent with a glossary.

On investigating the language of plants across the board, I also stumbled across the Doctrine of Signatures. Emerging in ancient Greece and explored further by European alchemists, herbalists and philosophers, this concept focuses on the idea that plants resembling human body parts can be used to treat problems in those matching body parts. Perhaps the most interesting and controversial form of humankind interpreting the natural world!

When determining which plant may benefit which organ, cues are given by form, texture and colour. Walnuts are said to benefit the brain, avocadoes the uterus, tomatoes the heart and grapes and berries the lungs. Ever looked closely at the sliced cross-section of a carrot? Does it look a bit like an eyeball? Even in my own little world, some plants hold a little magic and whimsy for me. Rosebuds and rosehips, raspberries on the cane, twiggy stems of wintersweet and tendrils of flowering jasmine both evoke fond childhood memories and a sense of ceremony when I bring them inside to enjoy.

On investigation, I have discovered that in the world of floriography, all things Rosa generally gravitate around affairs of the heart (with meanings differing depending on colour); raspberries hint at temptation or scornful beauty; wintersweet indicates faithfulness; and jasmine, cheerfulness and wealth. While much of this symbolism has fallen from mainstream thought, it does provide a fascinating insight into the influence of the natural world within human societies.

The sentimental garden

HOW PLANTS IMBED THEMSELVES IN OUR STORIES

Even though I didn't stay up to watch Queen Elizabeth's funeral, it wasn't long before I caught the chatter about the beautiful flowers that adorned her coffin.

To gardeners, her funeral wreath was obviously more than simply decorative, with the featuring of many humble and familiar garden plants that perhaps wouldn't normally be used in occasions of such pageantry. There were winding limbs of rosemary, a symbol of remembrance, and English oak, a representation of strength. Cut from the gardens of Buckingham Palace, Clarence House and Highgrove were garden roses, sedum, dahlias, scabious, pelargoniums and hydrangeas. Perhaps most sentimental was the addition of myrtle, grown from a sprig of the same plant used in the Queen's wedding bouquet from her 1947 marriage to Prince Phillip.

The inclusion of the myrtle pinged my heartstrings and got me thinking about how plants can anchor themselves in our memories and stories as much as places and material items can.

In my own family, my sister and I carried on the tradition of including snips of homegrown *Oxypetalum coeruleum* (tweedia) in our wedding bouquets. This began with our great-grandmother, before trickling through the generations to us. Including tweedia in my bouquet made me feel connected to my lineage, in particular to my grandmother, who died when my mother was only in her early twenties. I'm sure Mum felt this connection to her, too, while tucking tiny tweedia into her own bouquet just a few years later.

Recently a small group of us accompanied my gardening mentor Penny Zino (page 48) to her childhood property in North Canterbury with the specific aim to view the mature stand of native planting curated by her late mother, Brownie Davison, and now under the care of her brother and sister-in-law. We stalked its edges and explored the undergrowth, taking in many an extraordinary

Opposite: My homegrown wedding bouquet featuring tiny blue tweedia, as is our family tradition.

specimen and in turn, finding a thread of Brownie within it. Curation of planting can be very unique to its gardener, and I felt while exploring the paths that I was exposed to a little piece of Mrs Davison, whom I never met.

In its midst was a fantastical stand of the New Zealand native *Clematis paniculata*. Sprawling up and around surrounding trees, its gorgeous white, starry flowers glowed in the afternoon sun. This plant was an absolute favourite of Penny's mother and was the subject of many of her paintings, which are dotted around the homes of her children, as well as those of art collectors. Her passion for this clematis continued to capture the hearts of her family, with her daughter-in-law weaving it through her hair for her wedding day and Penny growing it prolifically in her own garden in an ode to her mother's memory.

Another close gardening friend of mine, Jenny Cooper (page 246), shared how she recently divided up some plants to send to her daughter on the Kapiti Coast, north of Wellington. This included a blue hosta that had belonged to her mother. 'My mum passed away ten years ago, and I know my daughter will cherish that this plant is also from me, even when I am gone,' shared Jenny. She is right in suggesting that this humble hosta has become a meaningful living heirloom, softly connecting generations.

Jenny also raised the idea that plants hold memories. She shared that the saxifrage she grows was given to her by an elderly woman she helped following the Christchurch earthquakes. To Jenny, that plant is inextricably linked to her and that life-changing event.

Plants can bear witness to our lives, and stopping to pay attention to who they are feels quite comforting to me. I felt true delight when moving into my first purchased home to discover a Japanese maple tucked away down the end of the garden. It was almost an exact replica of the one that grew outside the kitchen door at my childhood home near Hanmer Springs. Even now I look at its lovely multi-stemmed form and remember the hot summers of twisting ourselves through that earlier tree's limbs. I feel compelled to introduce grape hyacinths in the ground nearby in direct reflection of the planting my mother did over forty years ago.

Yes, it's true that plants hold memories. While it might only be the most sentimental among us (my hand is shooting up!) that attaches such human emotion to plants, they certainly are timeless, enriching bridges to our past – and perhaps easier to cope with than an enormous inherited sideboard!

Now might be just the right time to introduce a new botanical tradition to your own family story.

Below: The engaging native planting by my friend Penny Zino's mother.
Next page: Autumn dawn at the Christchurch Botanic Gardens.

My garden forgives me

IT'S NOT AS DEMANDING AS I THOUGHT

In the lead-up to Christmas one year, I found myself in a garden funk. I felt as though I had lost my grip on its activity and was feeling heavy under the looming deadlines of life and work that always seemed to present themselves at this time of year.

The reality of my situation rushed in as I slogged my way across my water-logged back garden following a week of very heavy rain.

Thanks to the disappointing absence of a stormwater connection off our picture framing studio, the lawn was totally submerged under a 'romantic', ankle-deep lake. Romantic was the only word I could come up with as I waded around lifting yet-to-be-planted punnets of seedlings off the ground as they threatened to float away in my bow wave. My thoughts were far from romantic, however, as I sighed deeply in guilt that these plants weren't yet in the ground. They were meant to be in weeks if not months ago. As were the strangled 'Limelight' hydrangeas that I bought in the autumn, forlornly looking back at me, still waiting for me to pull out the mountains of bear's breeches that stood between them and the garden. Still. Not. Done.

With housesitters due to arrive later that week, my guilt had led to fear. Fear that my visitors were readers of my gardening column, or followed me on social media and were about to have their summery visions of a happy, healthy garden unmet. To be fair, a good fifty per cent of the garden would have satisfied them, with my stacked vegetable garden turned perennial palace really coming into its own and the tall tops of my thalictrum budding into magnificence down the back. I even felt a little jealous that they would get to see my first echinacea pop into bloom.

Opposite: Even when underwater due to poor stormwater drainage, my garden is more forgiving than I give it credit for.

It's the other half that was as grim as a vacant lot, and unfortunately, this was the area immediately viewed out the living room window. It had been left to do anything it pleased behind the new arching lines of bricks indicating where the planned larger beds would be formed.

The hiccup had been in the waiting for trees to be removed and this had been delayed until January. I couldn't decide if it was worth the torture of my pressurised timeframe to tidy it up before then specifically to avoid outing myself to my guests as nothing more than a weed farmer! Even the deadheading of the iceberg roses at the front of the house had been left too late for my visitors to enjoy some bright new growth. The tiny strip of planting along the driveway fence had some underfed sweet peas trying to do their thing, along with falling-down scabiosa and two ragged-looking self-seeded hollyhocks. I was furious I didn't top it up with fresh soil and replant with finesse as I'd imagined I would last autumn. At this point, it appeared as a 'half garden', with sporadic planting intermingled with an infestation of fennel seedlings.

I truly, deeply love my garden and everything it offers me. Even the guilt, in a way, when I simply cannot keep up with the constant trudge forward of the seasons. Because I know that, despite my delays in doing its work, my garden will forgive me.

It forgave me when I didn't plant my spring bulbs until mid-winter. It also forgave me when I hurriedly and roughly dug up huge clumps of dahlias, moving them without dividing them into soggy, cold soil in wintery August. Everything still flowered and survived.

It forgives me when I forget to water the pots, sending wilty warning shots just in time for me to revive them, or when I procrastinate on feeding the eternally fruiting, potted limequat that waves its yellowing leaves in protest.

My garden offers me the opportunity to care for something living outside of myself, my husband and my cat. Unlike the mammals that would decline rapidly if I chose to turn my back on them and their survival needs, the garden always seems to say 'Don't worry, it's never too late for me'.

I really do marvel at the fact that with some concentrated time and effort, I know that I can rescue all the areas and specimens that have been neglected over the year. That the vision I have for my special little haven can still be achieved, despite my wobbly efforts and juggling of time.

On advice from a book I read, I have made a habit of wandering out and lying spread-eagled on the lawn just before bedtime. Digging my fingertips into the ground and feeling the weight of my body on the earth, I listen to the rustle of leaves set against distant police sirens and my local boy racers, relaxing in intense gratitude that I have this place of refuge amid the chaos. Even when the black nightshade glares at me from its spreading patch, my garden remains on my team, no matter the attention (or lack of) that I give it.

How incredibly lucky I am.

Below: My husband, T, and Tonka the cat enjoying a quiet moment on our back patio.

The garden is a refuge

FINDING CALM, JOY AND SOLACE IN THE GROUND

We've all experienced times in life when the world around us feels surreal, stressful, too cruel and too hard. In response, we search for escapism to momentarily block it all out and take a breath. Before I took up gardening, my response to stress would have been exploring the hidden gems section on Netflix. But when the first of the Covid lockdowns were announced in New Zealand, I found myself nodding in agreement with everyone who declared 'I'm off to the garden'. I knew, too, that there is no better place to empty the mind and find refuge.

On writing to some of my growing mentors and asking them how their gardening passion had benefited their life, by and large, every reply, no matter how brief or lengthy, returned the same general response. Collectively, they spoke of the therapy found in caring for their plants, and the satisfaction of the resulting produce and atmosphere – all resting on the profound positivity of connecting with nature.

I could easily relate to their descriptions of walking barefoot in spring dew, in enjoying the birdsong and bee activity within the habitats they had created, and in playing witness to the blooming of plants and the shifting of seasons. The delicious feeling of being physically sapped at the end of a productive day spent outside was mentioned by all. Words like saviour, gratifying, joy, creativity, order, healing, education, rewarding, renewal and happiness floated from these accounts. If I were to summarise these gardeners' enthusiastic reports, it was that they had found their source of calm.

Reassured that my response to gardening matched those of my heroes, I decided to look further into the concept of nature providing comfort and healing to human minds.

Comprehensively covering this view is the book *The Well Gardened Mind: Rediscovering Nature in the Modern World*, by Sue Stuart-Smith,

Opposite: My garden provides so many opportunities for distraction and sanctuary.

a psychiatrist, gardener and wife to one of the UK's most revered landscape architects and garden designers, Tom Stuart-Smith. Stuart-Smith writes: 'Gardening is unusual in the extent to which it encompasses the emotional, physical, social, vocational and spiritual aspects of life.' I have turned over enough of its pages to be a librarian's worst nightmare, finding myself nodding in agreement to every point Sue presents. I agree because, through my own gardening experience, I now feel that I 'know'.

Other books focus on the rewards of nature and gardening, too. Derek Jarman's diarised account in his book *Modern Nature* shares his story of creating a garden in an extremely desolate environment, searching for solace in response to his devastating HIV diagnosis and eventual decline with AIDS. *War Gardens: A Journey Through Conflict in Search of Calm* by Lalage Snow profiles the force of the human spirit in seeking to create space and find nature even under repression and threat. And Willow Crossley's *The Wild Journal: A Year of Nurturing Yourself Through Nature* is an accessible seasonal guide to connect with nature through simple, sometimes creative, sometimes mindful activities.

I gratefully inched my way through these books because they reinforced what I had already discovered. They are written by gardeners who, like me, and probably you, 'get it'. They'd be preaching to the converted if it was only other gardeners they were writing for, but it's become obvious to me that it's not. Like me, in writing my column and books, they want to pull back the curtain on the wonders of gardening for anyone who'll listen. These are the books to leave like a dangling hook on the bedside table of your spare bedroom, or surreptitiously gift as a Christmas prezzie to non-gardening friends and family.

My own experience with the emotional effects of gardening came during my three years of battling infertility. At times I howled at the moon in disappointment from my midnight lawn. My lovely garden allowed me to ride the rollercoaster of what really is one of life's true mysteries! It provided a place for my husband and I to meet in all the ups and downs of our journey as normal life happened around us.

It's only in hindsight that I have realised that the physical tasks of planting, weeding and mulching were so positively consuming that any racing thoughts were entirely blocked out. I simply did the work and the focus remained there, offering brilliant and rewarding moments of reprieve with immediate results. It was moving meditation, and I had a sense of control that was missing elsewhere in my life at the time.

In early 2020, my gardening life matched my personal and professional life in many ways.

The day I witnessed pages of my first book *Petal Power* roll off the press was the day I had lessons on how to inject IVF hormones. The day I held my first completed book in my hands (a lifelong dream) was the first day I injected myself – in what I hoped would lead to another lifelong dream. The weekend I acted as host of a gardening panel at a large horticultural festival was the first weekend after the dismal failure of that fertility treatment.

After we made the difficult but right decision to not pursue further IVF and instead get on with our good life as a family of two, I launched myself into photographing and writing my next book, *Flowers for Friends*. This flower-filled immersion into part of my extended gardening life absolutely distracted me and softened the blow of changing my life course.

The more I consider the benefits of gardening, the more strongly I feel that bigger and better don't equal more joy. Just having something to care for seems to be the power in it all.

My gar

My mixed perennial and grass borders in late summer, less than twelve months after being planted out.

len

WITH JULIA
ATKINSON-DUNN

Diary of a garden transformation

Over the past six years, my urban backyard has taken me on a journey of gardening discovery, and in the process, I have attempted to rid it of boring static evergreen planting in pursuit of creating a wild, seasonally responsive refuge.

I've spent much time studying naturalistic gardens and the ideas around climate-resilient planting. Taking inspiration from my existing raised bed full of airy perennials, I spent more than a year cross-checking species I already loved for their hardiness, flowering times and water needs, while continually adding new ones to my wish list. After many garden visits and much quizzing of experts, it finally became my own aim to create beautiful planting combinations that were still resilient and required minimal additional water. The challenge was on!

To realise my planting dream, some big decisions and prep work were required and the resulting process was a little jerky as I procrastinated over the moves that needed to be made. I needed both more light and more space, with the pathway to this being the removal of a number of trees (paired with a loss of privacy!), the reclamation of lawn, the addition of new edging and a raised brick planter. Pushed along by my handy and extremely productive brick-laying husband, I was forced to be brave and commit to the pursuit of ideas that had only existed in coloured pencil in my notebook.

With some valuable visits from my knowledgeable garden friends and the creative use of hoses to map out garden borders, we ripped the band-aid off and got to work. By autumn 2022 the beds were cleanly established and it was time for the plants to go in. It was both incredibly confronting and exciting to be working with such a clean slate and I can admit to hours spent stabbing colour-coded bamboo stakes in the earth, attempting to translate my basic, not-to-scale

Opposite: T completing work on the new extended beds that have reclaimed lawn.

sketched plan at ground level.

This clear expanse also allowed me to plan and plant for all seasons of the year at once. Having always had a bit of a lacklustre spring garden, I was able to plant bulbs at the same time as my young perennials. I also got the chance to shift around my existing topiary balls to provide some fun for late winter when the majority of the planting would be dormant, and visually support the lower spring specimens as they emerged. The trees, topiary and brick structural elements were the skeleton of this garden, fading into the background during the height of the summer show, before re-taking the baton in the quiet months.

As a former interior designer, visualisation has always been a strong skill of mine, but it was a tricky task to imagine the progressive rise and fall of my planned planting through each season based on flowering times. Nonetheless, I put one baby gardener foot in front of the other and twelve months later, on reflection, I can honestly say that I'm quite proud of the outcome.

Early spring had me sweating a little about my plant spacing. Perhaps I was too cautious and I had simply created a sparse sea of singular plant 'boats' instead of the tightly packed flotilla I was after. But by mid-spring my worries were allayed – the reassuring, bolstering clumps of perennial foliage relaxed into the gaps. The early daffodil population was potentially a little low for the abundance I had imagined but I was thrilled by the fresh bushy plants of the early-flowering white *Penstemon* 'Snow Storm', the aquilegia varieties and the gorgeous butter yellow spears of *Sisyrinchium striatum* combined with the *Iris* x *hollandica* 'Blue Magic'. The best characters of all were the islands of *Phlomis russeliana*, which delivered a level of whimsy and graphic shape that underlined the fun and creativity I was attempting to capture.

Opposite above: Bamboo sticks with colour-coded tape helped me transfer my planting plan from sketch to garden. **Opposite below:** The new beds in very early spring.

Late spring was a lumpy sea of dense green dotted with yellows, whites and the icy blue of the ixia, which was strong and upright as opposed to its white sister, which simply fell over under flower. New colour emerged with the thick, tall stands of violet *Verbena bonariensis* taking hold and slowly, the *Oenothera lindheimeri* (formerly known as *Gaura lindheimeri*) began to open. A challenge was presented when I noticed the gaura in the raised planter thrive while the specimens in the ground grew leggy and snapped at the base under the weight. On research, I realised that my clay-based earth may not be as free draining as gaura required, so I removed a couple of plants and then cut the rest back strongly by two-thirds.

Shifting through early to mid-summer really pumped up my gardening confidence. The beds were thriving and gaining height and the colour palette had certainly shifted. A highlight was the cluster of *Coreopsis verticillata* 'Moonbeam' that glowed from the edge of the garden, yet the singular plants, popped in amid stronger neighbours, had sulked, withered and died. A lesson learned that it likes room and no foreign friends!

Yet, I also felt I had an oversupply of white. The airy fountains of gaura (which had reacted very well to its cut back) were attractively dotted with heads of crimson *Knautia macedonica* and the strong lipstick-pink petaled cones of echinacea were helping to break it up, but I needed more punch.

Opposite above & below: The early spring show of aquilegia and Dutch iris are slowly replaced by phlomis, ixia and bolstering clumps of summer perennials as the season progresses.

So I searched high and low to source some new shapes and colours in the form of *Salvia nemorosa* 'Caradonna' and *Penstemon* 'Garnet', which both possess a vertical form that could combat all my very delicate bobbly blooms. While only a few plants were injected, I am rubbing my hands together with the prospect of dividing and increasing my stock for the seasons ahead.

By late summer, the beds had reached full fairy-tale tangle.

Despite some precarious leaners and gaura swallowing up many of its neighbours, the wildness had a romance I had neither fully envisioned nor knew that I would relish so much.

As I hit the twelve-month anniversary of these beds I felt overcome with joy by the addition of grasses to my planting for the first time. *Miscanthus sinensis* 'Morning Light' had been a beautiful and sensible supporting act to the flowering perennials since late spring, with its gradually increasing grassy clumps and ethereal pale green leaves.

As the summer plants formed their seedheads, the miscanthus, now with its tall tufted fans and the gossamer heads of *Calamagrostis brachytricha* had taken the baton. Their flowers opened and softened with the cooling season and brought a whole new movement to the beds – a soft strength and feeling of intention amid the fading colour. I have plans to introduce more grasses in the future with an eye on the very upright structure and honey-coloured spikes of *Calamagrostis* x *acutiflora* 'Karl Foerster'.

There is still more evolution to come and many question marks hang over my choices. Will the beds artfully crisp up into a tonal land of seedheads and sculptural limbs? Or will the local climate instead leave it melting and mushy? Time will tell!

Nevertheless, the ever-present element of the unknown and personally pleasing results have been a brilliant distraction from the boring stresses of adult life. Once my plants were in the ground I felt free to adopt the eventual style as my own instead of deliberating over the principles of the New Perennial Movement (page 174). As a visiting friend pointed out, she had never seen a garden like mine before, and while it is true that mixed perennial and grass planting is still finding a place here in New Zealand, I felt oddly vindicated that my six years of gardening had led to my own creative statement.

I can only imagine what the next six will hold.

Opposite above & below: Here you can see the new beds shifting in colour from verdant late spring to ethereal mid-summer. **Next page:** The welcome arrival of flowering miscanthus, which takes the baton into autumn as the other blooms begin to fade.

Once my plants were in the ground I felt free to adopt the eventual style as my own instead of deliberating over the principles of the New Perennial Movement.

MY PLANTING LIST

Below are the plants I feature to take the baton as the seasons progress in my garden.

LATE WINTER

Sparse with low shapes and low dots of colour.

- Daffodils
- Topiary balls – both *Lonicera nitida* and *Buxus sempervirens*
- Cut back clumps of grasses and perennials
- *Camellia sasanqua* (espaliered along fence in flower)

EARLY SPRING

Fresh, with whites, soft yellows, blue and low green clumps of foliage. Also, contributing cherry blossom.

- *Aquilegia vulgaris* 'Clementine White'
- *Aquilegia caerulea* 'McKana Hybrid' (in a primrose yellow)
- *Iris* x *hollandica* 'Blue Magic'
- *Phlomis russeliana* (in bud)
- Low emergence of green, summer-flowering perennial clumps

Next page left: The Avon River bordering the Christchurch Botanic Gardens in it's autumn glory. Next page right: Cool *Salvia uliginosa* (bog sage) amid the warm autumn tones.

MID-LATE SPRING

Knee-high clumps with a romantic, soft palette of pale yellow, pale blues, whites and interesting shapes.

- *Aquilegia caerulea* 'McKana Hybrid'
- *Phlomis russeliana* (in flower)
- *Sisyrinchium striatum*
- *Ixia* 'White'
- *Ixia elivira* 'Duck Egg Blue'
- *Penstemon* 'Snow Storm'

EARLY SUMMER

Emerging height and bulk with a gradual shift into a new palette of purples, pinks, rusts, white and pale yellow with focus on airy forms.

- *Sisyrinchium striatum*
- *Echinacea*
- *Knautia macedonica*
- *Sanguisorba officianalis*
- *Verbena bonariensis*
- *Salvia nemorosa* 'Caradonna'
- *Oenothera lindheimeri* gaura
- *Filipendula* 'Rubra'
- *Salvia* 'Amistad'
- *Penstemon* 'Snow Storm'

- *Penstemon* 'Garnet'
- *Stipa gigantea*
- *Phlomis russeliana* (foliage and seedheads)

MID-SUMMER
Airy but rich tapestry with a vigorous crescendo of summer perennials. Strong colour amid the dotty sea of white.
- *Penstemon* 'Garnet'
- *Penstemon* 'Snow storm'
- *Coreopsis* 'Moonbeam'
- *Sisyrinchium striatum*
- *Echinacea*
- *Knautia macedonica*
- Fennel
- *Sanguisorba officianalis*
- *Verbena bonariensis*
- *Salvia nemorosa* 'Caradonna'
- *Oenothera lindheimeri* gaura
- *Filipendula* 'Rubra'
- *Salvia nemorosa* 'Caradonna'
- *Salvia* 'Amistad'
- *Daucus carota* wild carrot
- *Pennisetum villosum*
- *Stipa gigantea*
- *Phlomis russeliana* (foliage and seedheads)

AUTUMN
A slow and staggered decline of colour is replaced with seedhead forms and plant structure. Highlights are the grasses in flower.
- *Stipa gigantea*
- *Miscanthus sinensis* 'Morning Light'
- *Pennisetum villosum*
- *Calamagrostus brachytrica*
- Japanese anemones
- *Oenothera lindheimeri* gaura
- *Penstemon* 'Garnet'
- *Verbena bonariensis*
- *Salvia nemorosa* 'Caradonna'
- *Salvia* 'Amistad'
- *Phlomis russeliana* (foliage and seedheads)
- *Camellia sasanqua* (espaliered along fence in flower)

Index

Page numbers in *italics* refer to photographs.

Thank you

It will be very obvious to all readers that these pages reflect the generosity of shared wisdom from many passionate gardeners in New Zealand. My discovery of gardening has been propelled forward by them and I am so incredibly grateful to all that I have crossed paths with.

To my garden friends Penny Zino, Jenny Cooper, Robyn Kilty and Jill Simpson, I can't thank you deeply enough for your time offered to me but must warn you, there will be many more hours and years of it ahead! You've got me for life!

To Jo Wakelin, Karen Rhind and Claire and Tom Gilroy, thank you for letting me wander, photograph and write about your planting at will. Your spaces are too interesting to be hidden away!

To Colleen O'Hanlon, I will forever appreciate the opportunity you gave me to have my own garden column in *Stuff*, despite my vast lack of experience. The research and learning that resulted have been driven by the deadlines and responsibility I have felt to our readers. It's made a far more well-rounded gardener out of me, too.

To our editor, Tessa King, your thoughtful touch and excellent suggestions made me groan in appreciation, knowing that each one simply made this book better for our reader (even when I thought I had finished my writing!). I felt we had a conversation throughout the whole process with your lovely comments in the editing column.

Opposite: my niece, Ada, in the early autumn garden. Next page: Summer perennials in the late afternoon sun.

To my husband T, you are the driving force behind our garden, pushing me forward when I am paralysed by indecision. Your productivity is unrivalled, as is your willingness to help bring my experiments to life. How did I get so lucky?

www.flaxmeregarden.co.nz / www.bluehouseamberley.nz
www.robynkiltygardens.co.nz / www.fishermansbay.nz

KOA PRESS

Published in 2023 by Koa Press Limited.
www.koapress.co.nz
@koapress

A Guided Discovery of Gardening
ISBN 978-0-473-67205-8

10 9 8 7 6 5 4 3 2 1

Publisher and Director: Tonia Shuttleworth
Editor: Tessa King @tessaroseking_editorial
Proofreader: Anna King Shahab @radish._
Poetry: Mary Walker @mary_walker_writer
Designer: Tonia Shuttleworth
Photographer: Julia Atkinson-Dunn
@studiohomegardening @studiohome
Cover and interior illustrations (pages 14, 102, 160
and 296): istock.com/ulimi

A catalogue record of this book is available from
the National Library of New Zealand.

Printed in China by 1010 Printing.